Heart of Briarwood

Katrina Case

© 2024

All rights reserved. No portion of this book may be reproduced without written permission from the publisher or author, except as permitted by U.S. copyright law.

Chapter One: A New Beginning

The bell above the door of Maggie's store, Hartwell Mercantile, tinkled softly as the morning sun streamed through the wide windows. The familiar scent of dried herbs, freshly stacked flour sacks, and the faintest hint of lavender filled the air. Hartwell Mercantile was the lifeblood of Briarwood, a place where anyone could find what they needed—whether it was sugar, a length of fabric, or just a kind word.

The store was sturdy, built from weathered oak, with a wide front porch where townsfolk often gathered to chat or rest. Inside, the shelves were neatly organized, everything in its place. Rows of jars filled with preserves, spices, and candy lined one wall, while tools and farming equipment sat ready for purchase along the back. Maggie had stocked the store herself, making sure to have everything from sewing needles to coffee tins.

Maggie Hartwell moved with practiced ease behind the counter, her black wavy hair tied back loosely to keep it out of her face. She wore a simple, practical gown in soft lavender with a faded apron tied over it. Her brown eyes, usually calm and composed, darted around the shop, ensuring everything was in place before the rush of customers came in for the day.

"Morning, Maggie," came a familiar voice from the doorway.

Maggie turned and smiled at the sight of Eliza Crenshaw, the elderly woman who had known her since childhood. Eliza's bonnet was slightly askew, and her smile was warm, though her sharp eyes missed little.

"Good morning, Mrs. Crenshaw," Maggie greeted with a smile, stepping out from behind the counter. "How are the boys?"

"Oh, they're well enough," Eliza chuckled, shaking her head. "But I'll be needing more sugar. Those grandsons of mine won't stop pestering me for pies."

Maggie grinned as she fetched the sugar.

"I'll get that for you. Maybe you should put them to work in the kitchen and let them make their own pies."

Eliza let out a hearty laugh. "Oh, Maggie, you know they'd turn the kitchen upside down. No, I think it's better to keep my hands on the rolling pin for now."

Maggie handed her the sugar with a soft smile. Eliza Crenshaw was one of the few people in town who never pried too much into Maggie's personal life, but she had an air of wisdom about her. If there was one person Maggie could trust with her thoughts, it was Eliza, though she rarely shared them with anyone.

"Well, you know where to find me if you ever decide to take a break from pies and grandsons," Maggie said, placing the sugar on the counter as Eliza fished out a few coins from her purse.

"You ought to take your own advice, dear," Eliza said, raising an eyebrow. "It's not right for a young woman like you to spend all her time here. You deserve more than just work."

Maggie's smile faltered for a moment, but she quickly recovered.

"Business keeps me busy, Mrs. Crenshaw. No time for much else." Eliza nodded knowingly but didn't press further.

As she gathered her things and left, Maggie turned back to her work, her fingers tracing the familiar surface of the wooden counter. The store was quiet again, save for the creak of the old oak floors and the occasional flutter of curtains from the open window.

Hartwell Mercantile was more than just a place to sell goods—it was Maggie's shield against the outside world. A place where she could control her destiny, far from the prying eyes of people like Edward Townsend, whose presence in town still lingered like a shadow she couldn't quite shake.

The sun had begun its slow descent behind the rolling hills as Maggie Hartwell stepped outside Hartwell Mercantile. She wiped her hands on her apron, then admired the quiet stillness settling over Briarwood. The soft golden light bathed the town, casting long shadows on the dirt road. A few people lingered, finishing their evening errands, but the town was winding down for the most part.

With a satisfied sigh, Maggie locked the store door, the familiar sound of the iron key clicking in place, bringing her a sense of calm. The weight of the day lifted from her shoulders as she turned and walked down the porch steps. Her house, a modest but comfortable cottage, lay just at the edge of town, a short walk from the store. As she walked, the sounds of crickets and the distant rustle of trees filled the air.

Maggie's boots scuffed softly against the dirt road, and she found herself appreciating the simple beauty of her routine. She had always found peace in the small things—closing her store, feeding her animals, and watching the sun set on another day. Arriving at her cottage, Maggie opened the wooden gate that led to her yard. The small house, framed by wildflowers and a white picket fence, stood under the shade of a large oak tree.

As soon as the gate creaked open, a loud bark pierced the stillness, and Bear, her loyal dog, came bounding toward her. Bear was a shaggy shepherd mix, his coat a mix of browns and blacks, and his tail wagged wildly as he reached her. Maggie knelt down, her face softening as she ran her fingers through his fur. "Hey, boy," she murmured, scratching behind his ears.

"Miss me?"

Bear responded with an enthusiastic lick to her cheek, his body practically excitedly vibrated. She laughed and stood, giving him a gentle pat.

"All right, let's get you some supper."

The cottage was cozy and warm, with wooden beams across the ceiling and a stone hearth that Maggie always kept well-tended. She grabbed Bear's bowl from the kitchen and filled it with leftover scraps and fresh meat, placing it down for him before turning her attention to the barn. The barn was small but sturdy, with a low wooden roof and large doors that creaked when opened.

Inside, her horse, Willow, greeted her with a soft whinny. Willow was a gentle bay mare with a sleek brown coat, her dark eyes watching Maggie as she approached.

"Good evening, girl," Maggie said softly, stroking Willow's neck.

She grabbed a handful of hay from the corner and laid it in the trough before filling her water bucket. Willow nuzzled her hand gently, a gesture of affection that Maggie had always cherished. As Willow ate contentedly, Maggie leaned against the barn door, watching the last rays of sunlight dip below the horizon.

The soft hum of the evening wrapped around her, and for a brief moment, everything felt right. Yet, in the quiet of the dusk, her mind wandered—back to the store, to the people she saw every day, and to the things she avoided thinking about. Edward still came around too often, his presence an unwelcome reminder of her past choices. Shaking her head, Maggie pushed the thoughts aside and focused on her peaceful evening routine. She wasn't ready to dwell on old wounds or new possibilities.

For now, it was just her, Bear, and Willow, and that was enough. As darkness fell over Briarwood, Maggie closed the barn doors and returned to the cottage, where the warmth of the hearth and the familiar comfort of her home awaited her. She couldn't help but smile as Bear padded beside her, curling up near the fireplace, his tail still wagging lazily. Tomorrow would be another busy day at the store, but tonight, Maggie allowed herself a few moments of quiet—just her and the world she had built, a world she controlled.

Chapter Two: The Quiet Storm

The morning air was crisp, a bite of coolness hinting at the changing season, and a light breeze rustled through the towering oaks lining the edges of Briarwood. Maggie Hartwell stood on the front porch of Hartwell Mercantile, the mug of coffee warming her hands. The world seemed to glow, bathed in the soft blush of dawn. Pink, lavender, and gold melted into one another across the sky, stretching over the horizon in painterly strokes. For a brief moment, Maggie let herself be still, eyes closed, absorbing the serenity of the early hour. At her feet, Bear lay sprawled across the wooden planks, his shaggy coat catching the amber light. His black and brown fur gleamed like polished stone, his massive head resting between his paws. The dog's tail thumped lazily as he glanced upward toward Maggie, his warm amber eyes full of silent loyalty. Maggie crouched down, gently scratching behind his ears, smiling as the breeze carried the scent of earth and fresh pine.

"Ready for another day, Bear?" she murmured.

His only response was a contented huff as he nuzzled her hand, eyes half-closed in contentment. Maggie rose and took in the view. Briarwood—her town, her home—stretched out in front of her like a beloved old quilt. It was worn in places patched up over the years, but it held warmth and comfort in every stitch. The wooden storefronts faded but sturdy, framed the dirt-packed streets, which led toward fields that disappeared into the horizon. Each building had a story to tell, just like the people within them. The bakery's window was already open, and she could faintly see Millie placing fresh loaves on the ledge to cool. The chipped and weathered schoolhouse stood proudly on the corner, where generations had learned their letters and lessons. And the church, with its white steeple piercing the sky, cast long shadows across the sleepy town in the afternoon sun.

This place was more than just home—it was a part of her, woven into the very fabric of who she was. The porch beneath her feet, the wooden sign swung gently in the breeze, the oak tree that had shaded her since childhood—it all carried memories. And with her parents gone, her duty was to carry those memories forward. Maggie lingered a moment longer before stepping back inside the mercantile. The sign above the door, Hartwell Mercantile, hung in its usual place, a testament to the legacy her parents had built. She took a deep breath, inhaling the familiar scent of wood, leather, and herbs. The store was as it always was—calm, orderly, and filled with life's little necessities. Shelves brimmed with flour, spices, fabrics, and tools, all carefully arranged in the same methodical order her mother had instilled in her from a young age.

Bear followed her inside, padding quietly as Maggie set her coffee mug on the counter. Her fingers lightly brushed the smooth wooden surfaces as she moved through the store, checking inventory. The morning's calm filled her with a sense of quiet pride. Every item on these shelves was a reflection of her hard work and her dedication to this place. This was her refuge from the chaos of the outside world. The steady rhythm of the day usually brought her peace. But today, a storm was brewing. She felt it in the air.

By midmorning, the town had fully awakened. The distant sound of horse hooves and the murmur of conversations drifted through the open windows. Mrs. Eliza Crenshaw shuffled into the store not long after, her bonnet askew, her sharp eyes twinkling with mischief. Maggie greeted her with a smile, the usual exchange of tea and gossip easing the tension in her chest. But that tension never fully left—it lingered like a shadow. The bell above the door chimed throughout the morning as the regulars came and went, offering brief moments of comfort. Yet even as the town bustled on, Maggie couldn't shake the feeling of unease. Something was coming.

It wasn't until the bell chimed again in the late afternoon that the source of her anxiety walked through the door. Edward. His presence filled the mercantile like a thunderstorm rolling over the plains—sudden, overpowering, and unwanted. His boots clicked across the wooden floor with a deliberate, measured rhythm, each step a reminder of the power he liked to wield. He wore his usual dark coat, perfectly tailored, his slicked-back hair gleaming in the afternoon light. His movements had a practiced elegance, a refinement that only made him more dangerous. Maggie didn't turn immediately. She didn't need to. She felt his eyes on her, felt the weight of his gaze like a pressure on her skin. Her grip tightened around the counter's edge, fingers trembling slightly despite remaining calm.

"Maggie," Edward's voice was smooth, the edges polished like stone, but the emptiness behind it was impossible to ignore. "Lovely afternoon, isn't it?"

She turned, meeting his gaze head-on, her brown eyes steady despite the storm brewing inside her.

"Afternoon, Edward," she said, her voice cold but polite, a shield she had perfected over the years.

He wandered through the store, his fingers trailing over the items on display with an unsettling familiarity as though he had a right to them. His presence felt invasive, each step violating the peace she had worked so hard to protect.

"You've always had a talent for running things smoothly," he commented, eyes scanning the shelves.

"Business seems to be thriving."

Her heart raced. The condescension in his words wasn't new, but it still crawled under her skin, setting her nerves on edge. His visits had become less frequent, but they were no less disruptive. He had a way of twisting compliments, turning them into weapons without ever raising his voice.

"Is there something you need, Edward?" Maggie's voice was steady, though she could feel her pulse pounding in her ears.

Edward paused, his smile faltering for just a second, but it returned quickly sharper this time. He leaned against the counter, far too close for comfort.

"Just checking in. After all, old friends should keep in touch, don't you think?" Maggie held his gaze, and her stare hard as stone.

She knew his game well—the subtle ways he tried to assert control, to remind her of the power he thought he still held over her. But she wasn't the same person she had been when they were together. She wouldn't let him manipulate her anymore.

"I'm busy, Edward," she said, her voice cool and final. "If you need nothing, I'd appreciate it if you'd leave."

Something shifted in his expression, the easy charm fading for a moment as his eyes darkened. He straightened his coat, stepping back from the counter.

"Of course," he said, his tone too sharp to be sincere. "I wouldn't want to get in your way."

With a tip of his hat, he turned and walked toward the door, the bell jingling as he left. But even as the door closed behind him, the storm he brought didn't leave with him. It lingered, a heavy weight in the air. Maggie's hands trembled as she reached down to pet Bear, who had padded over when Edward left.

"It's all right, boy," she whispered, though the words felt hollow. "He's gone."

But she knew better. Edward was never really gone. His presence lingered like the quiet before a storm, waiting, always waiting to return. This revision amplifies the atmosphere of tension between Maggie and Edward, highlighting the emotional undercurrents and deepening Maggie's internal struggle. It builds the contrast between the peaceful, predictable routine of her life and the chaos that Edward threatens to bring.

Chapter Three: The Gentle Arrival

The morning sun was brighter than usual as Maggie made her way to Hartwell Mercantile, a crisp, clean light that cut through the cool air. The slight chill of autumn had begun to creep into the mornings, the trees along Briarwood's main road tinged with hues of orange and red. Maggie smiled softly to herself as Bear trotted alongside her, his nose twitching at the scent of the fresh breeze.

Maggie unlocked the door to the store and let Bear wander inside. He made his usual loop around the store, sniffing every familiar corner, while Maggie moved behind the counter to start her day. The shelves were fully stocked, and everything was in its place—just as it should be. As she prepared for the day's customers, her thoughts wandered briefly to Edward's unwelcome visit from the previous afternoon. She shook her head, determined not to let his lingering presence darken her morning.

The bell above the door chimed, and Maggie turned with her usual smile, ready to greet the first customer of the day. But when her eyes landed on the tall figure that stepped inside, her breath caught ever so slightly. Daniel Whitaker stood in the doorway, his broad frame filling the small space as he removed his hat, revealing tousled dark brown hair. His sun-kissed skin bore the marks of a man who had worked the land for years, and his hazel eyes held a calm, steady gaze. He had a quiet presence—strong but without the overbearing confidence that Maggie had grown so wary of in others.

"Morning, Miss Hartwell," he greeted, his voice deep and steady as he gave a respectful nod.

There was no hint of assumption in his tone, no expectation of familiarity. It was simply a greeting, plain and simple. Maggie found her voice quickly, though the slight flutter in her chest surprised her.

"Good morning, Mr. Whitaker. What can I help you with today?"

Daniel smiled faintly, the corners of his eyes crinkling, making him seem even more approachable.

"I need a few things for the farm. I'd be mighty grateful for some nails, a length of rope, and if you've got any fresh bread left."

Maggie nodded and set to work gathering the items. As she moved around the store, she felt Daniel's eyes on her—not in a way that made her uncomfortable, but as though he was observing. There was something different about him, something that set him apart from the other men in town. He was quiet and thoughtful. He didn't fill the space with unnecessary words or loud gestures. When she returned to the counter with the items, Daniel leaned slightly against the wooden frame, his hat resting beside him. His hands—large and calloused—looked strong enough to move mountains, yet there was a gentleness about him, as though he was fully aware of the power he held and careful not to misuse it.

As Maggie rang up his items, Bear padded over, his nose twitching at the new visitor. Daniel knelt down to give the dog a friendly scratch behind the ears.

"That's a good-looking dog you've got there," he said, his voice warm with genuine interest. "What's his name?"

Maggie smiled, watching the easy interaction.

"Bear," she replied, her tone softening as she spoke of her loyal companion. "He's been with me a while now."

"Good name," Daniel said, standing again, his gaze meeting Maggie's once more. "You can tell he's well looked after."

Maggie felt her cheeks warm slightly, though she wasn't sure why. She cleared her throat and slid the parcel of goods across the counter.

"That'll be fifty cents for everything." Daniel reached into his pocket and placed the coins on the counter without hesitation.

He seemed in no rush to leave, and for a moment, the quiet between them was comfortable, like the gentle pause of a breeze.

"Looks like the store's doing well," Daniel remarked, glancing around the room. "It's good to see. This town needs places like this."

Maggie looked around her store, the pride she felt always swelling in moments like this.

"Thank you," she said softly, meeting his eyes again. "It's been a lot of work, but it's worth it."

Daniel's gaze lingered on her for a moment longer than expected, as if he could see more than just the store—like he could sense the weight she carried behind her calm exterior.

"Hard work pays off," he said simply, but the sincerity in his voice made it feel like more than just a platitude. He tipped his hat again, a slight smile on his lips. "I'll be by again soon, Miss Hartwell. Appreciate the help."

Maggie nodded, her heart stilling its flutter as she watched him leave. The door swung shut behind him, the bell chiming softly in the stillness of the store. For a long moment, she stood there, staring at the door. Something about Daniel Whitaker lingered in the air, like the faintest scent of a wildflower carried on the wind. He was different from the others in town, different from anyone she had known.

And as she turned back to her work, her mind continued to drift back to the quiet way he had looked at her—like he saw more than just the shop, more than just the woman running it. Maybe, she thought, her heart still wrestling with her mind, maybe there was more to Daniel Whitaker than she was ready to admit.

Chapter Four: Unexpected Help

The morning fog clung to Briarwood, the thick mist making the streets look like a watercolor painting in soft shades of gray and blue. Maggie stood just outside Hartwell Mercantile, frowning slightly as she eyed the large crates of new supplies that had been delivered earlier. They were heavier than expected—bulky shipments of tools, flour, and other essentials—and though Maggie prided herself on doing things on her own, the sheer weight of them gave her pause. She tugged at the corner of one crate, trying to shift it with a grunt of effort.

"Need a hand with that, Miss Hartwell?"

The deep, familiar voice caught her off guard, and she turned to see Daniel Whitaker approaching from the street, his wide-brimmed hat shading his face. His warm, hazel eyes held that same quiet intensity she had noticed the last time he was in the store. Maggie brushed her hands on her apron and straightened.

"I can manage," she said, though her cheeks flushed slightly from the effort.

Daniel's mouth twitched with the hint of a smile. "I don't doubt it. But it'd be no trouble for me to help."

He took a step forward, eyeing the crates thoughtfully. "Looks like quite a load."

Maggie hesitated. She wasn't used to accepting help. She wasn't sure she wanted to start. But something about Daniel—his calm, steady presence—made her consider it. After all, there was no harm in letting someone lighten the load, just this once.

"All right," she said finally, crossing her arms over her chest.

"But only because these are heavier than they look."

Daniel's smile widened slightly as he moved toward the crates. Without a word, he bent down and lifted one effortlessly, his muscles straining beneath his shirt. Maggie stepped aside as he easily carried the crate into the store, setting it down in the back near the supply shelves. Maggie followed, still slightly unsettled by how easily he had handled the weight that had given her so much trouble.

"Thank you," she said, her voice a little softer now. "I appreciate it."

"Glad to help," Daniel replied, returning for the next crate. "I'm heading back to the farm, but I saw the delivery outside and thought you might need a hand."

The two continued working together in a comfortable silence, with Maggie directing where each item should go and Daniel quietly obliging.

The sun slowly burned away the fog, and the day's warmth settled into the store as they worked side by side. As Daniel set down the last crate, he paused and looked around the shop, his eyes taking in the neatly organized shelves and the soft light filtering through the windows.

"You've built something real nice here, Maggie," he said quietly, his voice filled with genuine admiration. "It's not easy running a place like this all on your own."

Maggie blinked, caught off guard by the simple honesty in his words. She had heard compliments before, but something about the way Daniel said it felt different. Like he understood what it had taken for her to keep everything going.

"Thank you," she said softly, glancing around the store herself. "It wasn't easy. But it's worth it." She paused, then added, "I grew up here, you know. My parents started the store, and after they passed, it just… felt right to keep it going."

Daniel nodded, leaning slightly against the counter.

"That kind of dedication is rare these days. A lot of folks move on, looking for something bigger or better. But not you."

Maggie felt a warmth rise in her chest, but before she could respond, the sound of footsteps outside caught both their attention.

The door swung open, and there stood Edward Townsend, his expression darkening the moment his eyes landed on Daniel. Dressed impeccably as always, Edward's sharp gaze flicked between the two of them, and the tension in the room thickened almost instantly.

"Maggie," Edward greeted, his voice smooth but colder than usual. "I didn't expect to find you… entertaining guests so early in the morning."

Maggie straightened, the familiar unease creeping back into her chest. "Daniel was just helping me with some deliveries," she said, her tone steady, though the shift in the atmosphere was undeniable.

Edward's eyes lingered on Daniel, his mouth curving into a thin smile that didn't quite reach his eyes.

"How kind of you, Mr. Whitaker," he said, his voice dripping with false pleasantry.

"Though I imagine Maggie is more than capable of handling things herself."

Daniel's expression remained calm, though Maggie could sense the tension simmering just below the surface. He didn't rise to Edward's bait, simply nodding in acknowledgment.

"Just lending a hand, Mr. Townsend," Daniel replied evenly. "No harm in helping out when it's needed."

Edward's smile tightened, but he didn't push further. Instead, he turned his attention back to Maggie.

"I was actually hoping to speak with you today. Thought perhaps we could catch up—privately."

Maggie's stomach turned, but she kept her expression neutral.

"I'm busy, Edward. Perhaps another time." Edward's jaw clenched slightly, though he masked it quickly with another one of his polished smiles.

"Of course. Another time, then." He tipped his hat to her, casting one last glance at Daniel, before turning and leaving the store, the bell above the door chiming sharply as he exited.

For a moment, the store was silent, the tension still hanging in the air like the fading mist outside. Maggie let out a slow breath and turned to Daniel, who remained quiet but watchful.

"I'm sorry about that," she said, shaking her head. "Edward can be... persistent."

Daniel shrugged, his hazel eyes meeting hers with an easy understanding.

"No need to apologize," he said quietly. "I know the type."

Maggie studied him for a moment, then nodded.

"Thank you again for the help," she said, feeling a bit of the tension slip away as she spoke. "I appreciate it."

"Anytime, Miss Hartwell," Daniel replied, his voice warm but respectful as he tipped his hat. "You take care."

As he turned to leave, Maggie watched him go, the door closing softly behind him. The day outside had brightened, but inside the store, Maggie's thoughts were still clouded by the encounter with Edward. And yet, despite the tension that lingered from Edward's visit, Maggie found her mind drifting back to

Daniel—the quiet strength he had shown, the way he had helped without making her feel small. There was something about him, something she couldn't quite place.

For the first time in a long while, Maggie felt that maybe, just maybe, she didn't have to carry everything on her own.

Chapter Five: Treading Carefully

The late afternoon sun hung low in the sky, casting long shadows over the streets of Briarwood. The usual day bustle was quieting down, but Maggie was still out, making her way through the market with a basket of fresh produce tucked under her arm. The weight of her thoughts felt heavier than the basket she carried. She hadn't been able to shake the uneasy feeling since Edward's last visit—and it wasn't just Edward that had been on her mind.

As she moved through the stalls, nodding politely to a few townsfolk, her mind wandered back to Daniel. There was something about him—his calm, steady presence—that lingered with her even after he left the store. She felt a warmth toward him that she hadn't expected, but it came with a wave of hesitation. Letting someone in after what had happened with Edward… it wasn't something she was sure she could do. Just as she rounded the corner of the market, Maggie's eyes landed on a familiar figure.

Daniel Whitaker stood at a stall, speaking quietly with the vendor. His dark hair caught the fading light, and the sight of him standing there—tall, broad-shouldered, and unhurried—made Maggie's heart give an unexpected flutter. She slowed her steps, almost turning away, but before she could, Daniel looked up and spotted her. His expression softened immediately, a small smile tugging at the corners of his mouth.

"Afternoon, Miss Hartwell," he greeted, stepping away from the stall and walking toward her with easy, measured strides.

"Out for supplies?" Maggie nodded, lifting the basket slightly.

"Just picking up a few things before the day's done. And you? Stocking up for the farm?" Daniel glanced down at the sack of goods slung over his shoulder and shrugged.

"Same here. Thought I'd get a few things while the market's still open."

They stood there for a moment in comfortable silence, the sounds of the market softening around them as the evening crept in. Maggie wasn't used to this—small talk with someone who didn't seem to expect anything from her. With Edward, every conversation had felt like a transaction, a means to an end. But Daniel's presence was different. He wasn't trying to control the conversation or steer her in any direction. He was just… there. After a pause, Daniel shifted the weight of the sack on his shoulder and glanced at the basket in her arms.

"You need help carrying that back?" Maggie hesitated, instinctively ready to refuse.

She was used to doing things on her own—had always done things on her own. But then she looked at Daniel, saw the sincerity in his eyes, and something in her softened. Maybe accepting help wasn't a sign of weakness. She nodded, offering him a small smile.

"I wouldn't mind a hand, if you don't mind." Daniel reached for the basket, his fingers brushing hers lightly as he took it from her. "No trouble at all."

They walked together through the town, the rhythm of their steps falling in sync as they made their way back toward Hartwell Mercantile. The sun dipped lower, casting a soft golden light over the quieting streets. As they walked, Maggie found herself relaxing, the tension she'd carried all day slowly unraveling.

"Seems like things are busy at the store," Daniel said after a while, his voice low and easy. "You handle all that on your own?"

Maggie glanced up at him, the corner of her mouth twitching into a wry smile. "I manage. It's a lot of work, but I've never been one to shy away from it."

Daniel nodded, his gaze thoughtful.

"I can tell. Takes a lot of strength to keep something like that going."

Maggie felt a warmth spread through her chest at his words, though she quickly tucked it away. She wasn't used to praise that didn't come with strings attached. But with Daniel, it felt different—like he was seeing her for who she was, without any expectations. They reached the store, and Daniel set the basket down gently on the porch.

As Maggie opened the door, Daniel lingered for a moment, his eyes catching hers.

"I know you don't ask for help often," he said quietly, his tone steady, "but if you ever need it, you can count on me."

Maggie's breath caught for a second, the sincerity in his words sinking deep into her guarded heart. She nodded slowly, unsure of what to say but grateful for the offer.

"Thank you, Daniel," she said softly. "I'll... keep that in mind."

Daniel tipped his hat, a small smile still playing on his lips.

"You take care, Miss Hartwell."

As he turned to leave, Maggie watched him go, the warmth from his presence lingering long after he disappeared down the street. But just as she turned to step inside the store, her gaze landed on another figure standing at the corner of the street, watching.

Edward Townsend stood in the shadows, his eyes narrowed as he took in the scene that had just unfolded. His polished appearance was as pristine as ever, but there was something darker in his gaze—something calculating.

Maggie's heart sank as she realized that Edward hadn't just seen her with Daniel. He had witnessed something more—something that hinted at a growing connection she hadn't even fully processed herself. As Edward turned and walked away, the tension that had briefly lifted during her time with Daniel came crashing back down, heavier than before.

Maggie stood there for a moment, the door to the store still open, as the weight of it all settled on her shoulders. Edward wouldn't let this go. She knew that now. And as much as she wanted to ignore the tightening knot in her chest, she couldn't shake the feeling that Edward was going to make things more difficult. But she wouldn't let him control her. Not again.

Chapter Six: Crossing Lines

The late afternoon sun slanted through the windows of Hartwell Mercantile, casting long, golden beams across the floor. Outside, the streets of Briarwood were quiet, a soft breeze stirring the dust in the air. Maggie stood behind the counter, her hands steady as she restocked the shelves, though her mind was far from calm. It had been a few days since Daniel had helped her with the market, and she hadn't seen him since. She had thought about him more than she cared to admit—his gentle voice, the steady way he looked at her as if seeing past all the walls she had built around herself. And, of course, there was Edward. His constant, uninvited presence loomed in her thoughts like a shadow she couldn't shake.

The familiar chime of the shop's doorbell rang out, and Maggie's heart sank. She didn't even need to look up to know who had entered. She recognized the sharpness in the air, the way the atmosphere seemed to shift, charged with an unsettling energy.

Edward Townsend stepped into the store, his boots clicking slowly on the wooden floor. He was as immaculately dressed as ever, his dark coat spotless, his polished shoes reflecting the afternoon light. His face bore the same smooth, practiced expression that Maggie had come to despise—a mask of politeness that barely concealed the coldness underneath.

"Maggie," Edward greeted her, his voice like oil, thick and slick.

He smiled, but it didn't reach his eyes.

"I was starting to think you were avoiding me."

Maggie's grip on the shelf tightened, but she kept her voice steady.

"I've been busy, Edward. There's work to be done."

Edward's eyes flicked over her, assessing her as if she were another piece of merchandise in the store.

"So, I've noticed," he said, taking slow, measured steps toward the counter.

"I also noticed you've been keeping company with Daniel Whitaker."

The air in the room seemed to freeze, and Maggie's pulse quickened. Of course, Edward had seen her with Daniel. His gaze was sharper now, and his words edged with something darker than mere curiosity. Maggie straightened, turning to face him fully, refusing to be cowed. "Daniel was helping me with some supplies," she said, her voice clipped but calm.

"That's all." Edward's smile twisted into something more sinister, the thin veneer of charm slipping away. "Is that all it was, Maggie?"

His tone was low, almost mocking.

"Just help?" Maggie felt her heart thudding in her chest, anger bubbling up inside her. She had been patient with Edward for too long, allowing him to think he still had some hold over her. But this—this was too much. She stepped forward, her chin lifting as she met his gaze with fire in her eyes.

"What are you implying, Edward?" she asked, her voice sharper now, laced with steel.

Edward's smile faltered, and for a brief moment, something darker flickered in his eyes.

"You know, Maggie, I've been patient. I've been understanding. But I won't tolerate being humiliated."

"Humiliated?" Maggie's voice rose slightly, disbelief and anger coursing through her veins.

"You're not humiliated, Edward. You're obsessed. You think you can control me—well, you can't. Not anymore."

Edward's expression darkened, the pleasant façade slipping further as his eyes narrowed. He took another step toward her, his presence looming, oppressive.

"You think Daniel Whitaker can protect you? You think he understands you better than I do?"

Maggie's breath hitched, her heart racing. For a moment, she thought about stepping back, about retreating. But then, something shifted inside her—a fire, a strength she hadn't felt in a long time. She stood her ground, her eyes blazing with defiance.

"Daniel respects me," she said, her voice firm. "Something you've never done."

The silence that followed was thick and heavy. The air between them charged with tension. Edward's lips twisted into a sneer, and for a second, Maggie thought he might say something cruel—something meant to cut her down. But before he could speak, the door to the store swung open, and the familiar chime of the bell cut through the tension like a knife.

Daniel Whitaker stood in the doorway, his broad frame silhouetted against the afternoon light. His hazel eyes immediately locked onto Edward, and though his expression remained calm, there was a subtle shift in his posture—a readiness that made the air crackle with unspoken tension.

"Is everything all right here, Maggie?" Daniel asked, his voice low and steady, but there was an edge to it, a protective undercurrent that made Maggie's heart steady itself.

Maggie let out a breath she hadn't realized she'd been holding, the tension in her chest easing slightly at the sound of Daniel's voice. She glanced at Edward, whose eyes had darkened with something that looked like anger—or jealousy.

"Everything's fine," Maggie said, her voice stronger now, "Edward was just leaving."

Edward turned to face Daniel fully, and the two men stared at each other for a long, tense moment. There was something dangerous in the air, something volatile that made the room feel smaller, tighter. Edward's smile returned, though it was sharp and humorless.

"Of course," he said, his voice dripping with disdain. "I wouldn't want to overstay my welcome."

He tipped his hat to Maggie, though the gesture felt more like a warning than a courtesy. "Until next time," he added, casting one last, cold glance at Daniel before turning and walking out the door, the bell jangling behind him.

For a long moment, the store was silent, the air heavy with the remnants of Edward's presence. Maggie let out a slow breath, her hands still trembling slightly from the confrontation. She had never seen Edward like that before—so angry, so possessive. It unnerved her, but she refused to let him intimidate her. Daniel stepped forward, his eyes softening as he looked at her, concern etched into his features.

"Are you all right?"

Maggie nodded, though the tension still clung to her like a second skin. "I'm fine. He's just… persistent."

Daniel's brow furrowed, his jaw tightening as he glanced toward the door where Edward had just left.

"He shouldn't be coming around here like that. If he's bothering you—"

"I can handle it," Maggie interrupted, her voice firm but not unkind. She met Daniel's gaze, her heart softening at the concern in his eyes. "I've been handling it."

Daniel didn't argue, but his expression remained serious, his hazel eyes searching hers.

"I know you can," he said softly. "But you don't have to do it alone."

Maggie's heart skipped a beat at his words, a rush of warmth spreading through her chest. She wasn't used to hearing that—wasn't used to someone offering to share the burden she had carried for so long. But with Daniel standing there, steady and sincere, she wanted to believe him.

"I appreciate that, Daniel," she said quietly, her voice softer now. "I really do."

Daniel nodded, his expression softening.

"Anytime, Maggie."

They stood there in the store's quiet, the tension from Edward's visit slowly fading, replaced by a calm that felt almost foreign to Maggie. For the first time in a long time, she didn't feel quite so alone.

As Daniel turned to leave, offering her one last reassuring smile before stepping out into the golden light of the afternoon, Maggie watched him go, her heart still fluttering in the wake of his kindness. But just as she began to relax, she caught a glimpse of movement from the corner of her eye.

She turned, her heart sinking as she saw Edward standing at the corner of the street, half-hidden in the shadows. His eyes were fixed on her, dark and unblinking, and though his face remained expressionless, something in his gaze sent a chill down her spine. Maggie's stomach twisted. She had thought Edward would leave her alone after today, but now she wasn't so sure. There was something dangerous about how he looked at her—something possessive like he still believed he had a claim on her.

As Edward turned and disappeared down the street, Maggie stood in the doorway of her store, the weight of the moment settling on her shoulders. She had fought too hard to build her life in Briarwood, and she wasn't about to let Edward Townsend take that away from her. But as she watched the sun dip lower in the sky, casting long shadows over the quiet town, Maggie couldn't shake the feeling that the storm was far from over.

Chapter Seven: Close Encounters

The morning sun hung low in the sky, casting a soft, golden light over the streets of Briarwood. Maggie had just finished organizing a new shipment at Hartwell Mercantile, wiping her hands on her apron, when the familiar jingle of the shop's bell cut through the stillness. She glanced up and felt a rush of warmth in her chest as Daniel entered the store, his broad frame filling the doorway like a steady force.

"Good morning, Maggie," Daniel greeted, his voice low and reassuring, the kind that seemed to settle the air in the room.

His hazel eyes caught hers, and she found herself smiling despite the tension that had lingered in her since the previous day's encounter with Edward.

"Good morning, Daniel," she replied, her voice softer than usual, though a smile tugged at her lips. "What brings you in today?"

Daniel stepped forward, his boots thudding softly against the floor as he approached the counter.

"Just need to pick up a few things for the farm," he said, glancing around the shop.

"Nails, rope, the usual."

Maggie nodded, already familiar with what Daniel typically needed for his work. She moved behind the counter, gathering the supplies efficiently, but she couldn't help noticing how comfortable she felt with Daniel around. His presence was calming in a way she hadn't experienced in a long time. As she handed him the items, their hands brushed for a fleeting moment. It was a brief, simple touch, but it sent a warmth through Maggie that caught her off guard. She quickly pulled her hand away, her heart giving an unexpected flutter.

"Thank you," Daniel said, his voice a little quieter, his eyes briefly lingering on her before he took the supplies. They stood there for a moment, the silence between them not uncomfortable but charged with something unspoken, something that neither of them seemed quite ready to address.

Before either of them could speak again, the door to the shop creaked open once more, and the familiar weight of unease settled over Maggie as Edward stepped inside. The air in the store grew tense, the easy warmth of moments before evaporating in an instant. Edward's polished boots clicked against the wooden floor, his sharp gaze immediately landing on Daniel. His presence filled the room, but not in the reassuring way Daniel's did—Edward's presence felt suffocating, like a storm cloud looming overhead.

"Maggie," Edward greeted, his voice cold and clipped. "I didn't expect to find you so... busy."

Maggie straightened, her heart beginning to race. She could feel the tension building, the invisible line that had been drawn between Edward and Daniel now sharper, more dangerous. She glanced at Daniel, who stood calm and composed, though there was a flicker of quiet protectiveness in his eyes.

"Just helping out a customer, Edward," Maggie said, her voice steady despite the knot forming in her stomach. "What can I help you with today?"

Edward's lips curled into a thin, humorless smile as his eyes darted toward Daniel.

"It seems you've found yourself a new helper," he said, his tone dripping with condescension.

Before Maggie could respond, Daniel stepped forward, his tall frame blocking some of Edward's view of her. His hazel eyes were calm, but there was a firmness in his voice when he spoke.

"Just picking up some supplies, Mr. Townsend. Nothing more."

Edward's smile faltered, and for a brief moment, something dark flickered in his gaze. He took a slow step closer, his posture tense.

"You seem to be spending quite a bit of time here, Whitaker. Something keeping you in town?"

Maggie's heart tightened in her chest. The exchange between the two men felt like a coiled spring, ready to snap at any moment. She could see the barely concealed tension in Edward's stance, the jealousy simmering beneath the surface.

But before things could escalate further, Maggie stepped around the counter, determined to diffuse the situation. She couldn't allow Edward to intimidate her, and she wouldn't let him cause trouble for Daniel either.

"Edward, if you need something, I'll be happy to help," she said, her voice firm, though her pulse quickened. "But I think it's time you left."

Edward turned his gaze back to Maggie, his eyes narrowing.

"Is that how it is now, Maggie?" he asked, his voice low, dangerous. "You'd rather spend your time with the likes of him than with me?"

Maggie's temper flared. She had had enough of Edward's possessive behavior, enough of his attempts to control her life. She took a step forward, meeting his gaze with fire in her eyes.

"I'll spend my time with whomever I choose, Edward. You don't own me, and you never will."

The words hung in the air, sharp and final, cutting through the tension like a blade. For a long moment, Edward said nothing, his face a mask of barely controlled anger. His eyes flashed with something darker, something possessive and cold. But then, as if realizing he had lost this particular battle, Edward forced a sneer onto his lips.

"We'll see about that," he said quietly, his voice laced with menace.

He turned on his heel and stormed out of the shop, the bell above the door jangling violently as it slammed shut behind him. Maggie let out a shaky breath, her hands trembling slightly from the confrontation. She hadn't expected things to escalate like that, but she was glad she had stood her ground. Daniel's voice broke through the heavy silence, calm and steady.

"Are you all right?" Maggie nodded, though her heart was still racing. "I'm fine," she said, her voice steadier than she felt. "He's just... he's not used to hearing 'no.'"

Daniel's brow furrowed, concern clear in his expression.

"He shouldn't be coming around here like that. If he keeps bothering you, Maggie, you let me know."

There was something protective in his tone, something that sent another wave of warmth through Maggie. She hadn't expected him to step in the way he had, and for a moment, she felt a sense of relief that she hadn't felt in a long time—like maybe she didn't have to fight these battles alone anymore.

"I appreciate that, Daniel," she said softly, her eyes meeting his with gratitude. "Really."

Daniel gave her a small, reassuring smile, but there was still a flicker of tension in his eyes.

"Anytime." As he turned to leave, Maggie watched him go, the door swinging softly behind him.

For a moment, she stood there, the lingering sense of unease from Edward's visit gnawing at the edges of her mind. But the warmth from Daniel's words, his presence, stayed with her. She wasn't sure what was going to happen next, but for the first time in a long time, she didn't feel so alone.

Chapter Eight: A Familiar Face Returns

The afternoon sun beat down gently on Briarwood, casting soft light over the quiet streets. Maggie had just finished organizing a new shipment when the familiar jingle of the bell echoed through the store once again. She glanced up, expecting a regular customer, but froze when she saw the figure standing in the doorway. A woman about Maggie's age, with a cascade of auburn curls and a smile that hadn't changed in all the years since they were children, stood there with one hand still on the door. Clara Adams.

The childhood memories of summers spent running through the fields, and long talks on the porch flooded back instantly. But Maggie hadn't seen Clara in years—not since Clara left Briarwood for what seemed like a bigger and brighter future.

"Clara?" Maggie said, her voice barely above a whisper, still unsure if she was imagining things.

Clara's smile widened, her bright green eyes sparkling with recognition.

"Maggie Hartwell, as I live and breathe!"

Before Maggie could fully process the moment, Clara was across the room, pulling her into a tight, familiar embrace. Maggie was caught off guard and hugged her back, overwhelmed by the flood of emotions. It had been so long since she'd felt such warmth from a friend.

"What are you doing here?" Maggie asked as they pulled apart, her eyes scanning Clara's face for answers.

"I thought you'd never come back to Briarwood."

Clara sighed, a shadow passing over her expression, and for the first time, Maggie noticed the slight tiredness in her eyes.

"I'm back to take care of my father," she said, her voice softening. "He's not doing too well."

Maggie's heart sank at the news. She remembered Mr. Adams as a kind, strong man who had always been the heart of Clara's family.

"Oh, Clara, I'm so sorry. How is he?" Clara shook her head, forcing a small smile. "He's holding on, but it's been hard. He asked me to come back, and well… here I am."

Maggie reached out, placing a hand on Clara's arm.

"If there's anything I can do to help, you just let me know. I mean it."

Clara's eyes softened, and she gave Maggie's hand a squeeze.

"You've always been like that, Maggie. Always ready to help. I appreciate it."

They stood in comfortable silence for a moment, the weight of the years apart slipping away. It was like they had never been separated, as if the bond they shared as children had never truly faded.

"I can't believe you're back," Maggie said, shaking her head in disbelief. "It feels like just yesterday we were running around causing all kinds of trouble."

Clara laughed, her voice brightening for a moment. "

We were quite the pair, weren't we?"

They spent the next few minutes catching up, falling into an easy rhythm as they reminisced about their childhood antics and shared stories of the years that had passed. But as they spoke, Maggie couldn't help but notice how Clara occasionally glanced away, her smile faltering slightly whenever the conversation drifted toward the present.

Sensing there was more Clara wasn't saying, Maggie gently pressed, "So... you're back to care for your father, but how are you doing? I mean, really."

Clara hesitated, biting her lip as she looked down at the floor.

"It's... it's been hard," she admitted, her voice quieter now. "I thought I'd built a good life after leaving Briarwood. I was married for a while, you know. But things didn't work out."

Maggie's heart clenched at the sadness in Clara's voice. She hadn't known about Clara's marriage.

"I'm sorry to hear that. What happened?"

Clara sighed, brushing a stray curl behind her ear.

"Turns out I married a man who wasn't as kind as he seemed. When the marriage fell apart, I didn't know where to go. Coming back here... it felt like the only choice."

Maggie frowned, a mix of concern and sympathy swirling inside her. Clara had always been the more daring, adventurous one, the one who'd been eager to leave Briarwood behind and see the world. But now, standing in the store, she looked more fragile, more tired than Maggie had ever seen her.

"You're back now," Maggie said gently. "And I'm here. You're not alone in this."

Clara's smile returned, but it didn't quite reach her eyes.

"Thank you, Maggie. That means more than you know."

Just then, the door chimed again, and both women turned as Daniel walked into the store. His broad frame instantly filled the space. His eyes briefly flicked between Maggie and Clara, curiosity evident in his expression.

"Afternoon, Maggie," he said with a nod, then turned to Clara. "I don't believe we've met."

Clara's eyes widened slightly as she took in Daniel's appearance, her smile brightening in a way Maggie hadn't seen in a while.

"No, I don't believe we have. I'm Clara Adams, an old friend of Maggie's."

"Daniel Whitaker," he introduced himself, offering a polite nod. "Good to meet you, Miss Adams."

Maggie could feel a strange flutter of emotion as she watched the exchange, unsure of why she suddenly felt so… protective. Clara and Daniel exchanged pleasantries, but Maggie's mind was racing. Clara glanced at Maggie, her eyes twinkling mischievously.

"Well, Maggie, you didn't tell me you had such charming customers."

Maggie blushed, and Daniel, ever modest, simply chuckled and shrugged.

"I'm just here for supplies, nothing too exciting." Clara's teasing smile remained, but Maggie could sense a change in the atmosphere—one she wasn't quite prepared for.

"Well," Clara said, turning back to Maggie, "I should be going. I still have things to settle at my father's house. But I'll be by again soon. You can count on that."

Maggie nodded, her heart feeling easier now that Clara was back, though something new lingered in the air between them.

"You'd better. We have a lot of catching up to do."

As Clara left the store, waving one last time, Maggie stood there, her thoughts swirling. She couldn't help but feel that Clara's return would change everything—and she wasn't sure yet if she was ready for it.

Chapter Nine: A Dangerous Shift

The Briarwood Harvest Festival was a celebration the town looked forward to each year. Held during the last week of the harvest season, it was a time when the hard work of the farming community gave way to feasting, laughter, and a sense of unity. For generations, the festival had been a fixture in Briarwood's calendar, and for a small town like this, it was more than just a fair—it was a way to mark the passing of time, to reconnect with old friends, and to celebrate the end of another year's labor.

Colorful banners were strung between the wooden posts lining the town square, fluttering gently in the breeze. Stalls and booths crowded the streets, each packed with the harvest's fruits—bright red apples, jars of honey, and baskets overflowing with freshly picked vegetables. The rich, earthy scent of roasted meats mixed with the sweet fragrance of freshly baked pies, drawing in families from nearby farms and even a few out-of-towners who had heard of the festival's reputation. Children ran through the crowd, their cheeks flushed with excitement as they darted between the booths, laughing as they competed in sack races and three-legged contests. Their joy echoed through the square, adding to the energy that seemed to pulse through the heart of Briarwood.

Maggie stood at her booth near the center of the square, her stall neatly arranged with goods from Hartwell Mercantile. She and Clara had spent the morning setting it up—everything from bolts of fabric to jars of preserves and tools for the farmers. Clara had insisted on adding a few decorative touches, draping garlands of dried flowers along the edge of the booth to catch the eye of passersby.

"It looks wonderful," Maggie said, admiring the final result. "You've got a good eye, Clara."

Clara grinned, adjusting a bouquet of wildflowers.

"Well, someone's got to bring a little flair to the place. Can't let the farmers have all the fun."

As they finished preparing the booth, Maggie couldn't help but take in the festival around her. People came from every corner of Briarwood and beyond. Families from the surrounding farms—many of whom she'd known for years—walked hand in hand, smiling as they stopped at each booth to admire the goods or sample the food. Mrs. Crenshaw, with her crooked bonnet, was selling her famous blackberry jam from a nearby stall while the Millers offered freshly churned butter to anyone who passed by.

In the middle of the square, a group of fiddlers had taken to the makeshift stage, their lively music filling the air. Couples gathered near the stage, some preparing to dance while others stood tapping their feet, unable to resist the infectious rhythm. The laughter of the crowd, the music, and the vibrant colors created a sense of warmth and comfort that filled Maggie's heart. A few special events occurred each year, drawing even more excitement from the crowd. The pie-baking contest was always a favorite, with nearly every woman in town bringing their best recipe to be judged.

Today, the judges—local farmers with strong appetites—were already gathered, preparing to sample the endless pies laid out on the long wooden tables. Then there was the hog roast, which had been slow-cooking since dawn. The rich, smoky aroma wafted across the square, promising a hearty feast once the sun began to set.

It was a time-honored tradition, and families looked forward to gathering around the long tables, sharing food and stories as the evening wore on. Another tradition was the harvest king and queen, a title given to a local couple—usually the most successful farmers of the year. It was a lighthearted, symbolic way to honor the hard work of Briarwood's farming families, and the announcement was always a highlight of the evening.

Maggie's heart swelled with a quiet pride as she watched the people she'd grown up with—those she cared about—celebrate together. This was Briarwood at its best, a community coming together to share in the fruits of their labor. But even with the joy of the festival surrounding her, there was a nagging feeling that Maggie couldn't shake. As Clara chatted away, adjusting the display, Maggie's eyes wandered through the crowd, scanning for a familiar figure she hoped she wouldn't see.

Though full of life, the festival seemed to bring a sense of unease, and Maggie's thoughts drifted back to Edward. He hadn't been seen in the past few days, but the silence wasn't comforting—it was unnerving. Clara noticed Maggie's wandering gaze and nudged her gently.

"Maggie, relax. It's the Harvest Festival. Even Edward wouldn't dare cause a scene here, would he?" Maggie forced a smile, though her stomach twisted with unease.

"I just don't want any trouble today." Before Clara could respond, the booted footsteps drew Maggie's attention. Her heart lifted slightly as Daniel approached the booth, his familiar figure cutting through the crowd. Daniel's presence always seemed to settle Maggie's nerves—his calm, steady demeanor was a welcome contrast to the tension in her mind.

"Good morning, Maggie," Daniel said, his hazel eyes warm as they met hers. "How's the booth looking?"

Maggie smiled, grateful for his arrival.

"Clara's been adding her touches, so it looks better than ever."

Clara, ever the tease, grinned up at Daniel. "I'm just doing my part. Besides, I think things will go just fine with you around."

Maggie rolled her eyes, though the teasing felt lighter than usual. With Daniel here, the sense of safety she craved returned, but as the festival continued, Maggie's gaze drifted back to the crowd. She couldn't shake the feeling that something was about to happen. The festival-goers continued their merrymaking, oblivious to the storm brewing in the distance. Children laughed as they competed in the sack races and tug-of-war contests while couples danced to the fiddle music, their faces flushed with joy. The pie-baking contest was in full swing, with Mrs. Crenshaw looking confident as she stood by her creation, a towering blackberry pie that already had a few eager onlookers. But even as the festival thrived around her, Maggie's heart thudded with anxiety.

And then, just as she feared, she spotted him. Edward Townsend. His usual sharp appearance was gone, replaced by something more disheveled, more erratic. His clothes were wrinkled, his hair unkempt, and there was a wild look in his eyes that Maggie had never seen before. He moved through the crowd with a frenetic energy, his gaze locked on her, and Maggie's breath caught in her throat.

"Clara," she whispered, her voice barely audible over the festival sounds. "He's here."

Clara tensed immediately, her playful demeanor vanishing as she followed Maggie's gaze.

"Maggie, he doesn't look right. We should leave."

But it was too late. Edward had already seen them and was making his way toward the booth, his expression dark and dangerous.

Maggie's breath hitched. This wasn't the composed, arrogant Edward she had dealt with before—this was someone on the edge. Clara grabbed Maggie's arm.

"Maggie, he doesn't look right. We should go."

Before they could move, Edward reached the booth, his voice trembling with rage and desperation.

"Maggie… why are you doing this to me?" he shouted, loud enough for the nearby festivalgoers to stop and turn, their faces painted with confusion and concern.

Maggie's heart pounded as she stepped back, instinctively moving closer to Daniel.

"Edward, you need to calm down. This isn't the time or place."

But Edward wasn't listening. His face contorted with anger, and his voice grew louder, more unhinged.

"You've humiliated me! You've made a fool of me in front of the whole town!"

His words were slurred, his movements erratic. The crowd began to murmur, whispers spreading like wildfire. Festival-goers backed away, forming a wide circle around the scene, watching with shock and curiosity.

"Edward, please—" Maggie started, but before she could finish, Edward lunged toward her, his hands outstretched.

In an instant, Daniel was between them, grabbing Edward's arm and pulling him back with a firm, controlled strength. The two men struggled briefly, Edward thrashing in Daniel's grip like a wild animal.

"You're not going to hurt her," Daniel growled, his voice low and commanding.

The scene unfolded in what felt like slow motion. Several men from the town rushed forward to help Daniel restrain Edward, who continued to shout incoherently. His eyes were wild and unfocused as he struggled against the men holding him back.

"Let me go! I've done nothing wrong!" Edward screamed, his voice cracking. "She belongs to me! This is all her fault!"

At that moment, Sheriff Amos Turner arrived, pushing his way through the gathering crowd. Sheriff Turner was a tall, imposing man in his late forties with broad shoulders and a square jaw that had seen its fair share of trouble in

Briarwood. His gray eyes were sharp, always watching, always calculating. He wore a leather duster over his shirt, his badge gleaming in the late afternoon sun.

"Break it up, now!" Sheriff Turner barked, his voice cutting through the chaos. The men holding Edward stepped back slightly, gripping him as the sheriff approached. Edward twisted in their hold. His face flushed with rage.

"Sheriff! You're arresting the wrong man! I haven't done anything wrong!"

Sheriff Turner stepped forward, his gaze cool and unwavering as he assessed the situation. He glanced at Maggie, then at Daniel, before turning his attention to Edward.

"From where I'm standing, it looks like you've caused quite a bit of trouble, Townsend."

Edward's face twisted in disbelief.

"She's made a fool of me! Everyone's against me! You can't arrest me for defending myself!"

Sheriff Turner raised an eyebrow, unimpressed by Edward's rant.

"From what I've seen, the only one causing a scene here is you."

Edward's eyes widened with a crazed desperation.

"She's been turning the town against me! This whole thing is her fault!"

Sheriff Turner's jaw tightened, and he nodded toward the men holding Edward.

"Take him to the jail." "No!" Edward shouted, his voice cracking as he struggled against their hold. "I haven't done anything wrong! You'll regret this! All of you!"

As Edward was dragged away, still screaming, the crowd began to disperse, the whispers growing louder. Maggie stood frozen, her breath coming in short, shallow bursts. She hadn't expected things to spiral out of control like this, but the moment's intensity overshadowed the relief of seeing Edward taken away. Sheriff Turner turned to face Maggie, his expression softening slightly.

"You all right, Miss Hartwell?"

Maggie nodded, though her voice was shaky when she spoke.

"I... I didn't think it would come to this."

The sheriff's eyes were filled with quiet understanding. "I'll keep him locked up for now, but if you want this to go further, you'll need to make a formal complaint."

Maggie swallowed hard, her mind racing. The idea of pressing charges against Edward hadn't occurred to her until now. But she wasn't sure she had a choice with how things escalated. Daniel, who had remained quietly by her side, placed a reassuring hand on her arm.

"Whatever you decide, Maggie, we're with you."

Maggie looked up at him, her heart steadying at the warmth in his voice. She turned back to the sheriff, her resolve strengthening.

"I'll make the complaint, Sheriff. I'm not going to let this continue."

Sheriff Turner gave her a respectful nod.

"Good. Come by the office later, and we'll get it done."

As the sheriff walked away, the festival slowly began to resume, though the festive atmosphere was tinged with an air of unease. People continued to whisper, casting glances toward Maggie and Daniel as they stood together near the booth. Clara stepped forward, her expression a mix of concern and pride.

"I knew he was trouble, but I didn't think it would go this far."

Maggie nodded, still processing everything that had happened.

"Neither did I."

But as she stood there, surrounded by the lingering tension of the day, Maggie felt a sense of relief. Edward was gone—at least for now—and with Clara and Daniel by her side, she knew she could face whatever came next.

Chapter Ten: After the Storm

The soft chime of the shop door barely registered in Maggie's mind as she sat behind the counter, staring blankly at the ledger in front of her. The numbers swam before her eyes, but she couldn't focus. Even though Edward was now locked away, the weight of everything that had happened at the festival hung over her like a storm cloud that refused to pass. She hadn't expected things to escalate the way they had. Edward's wild-eyed, frenzied attack still haunted her.

Despite Daniel's quick intervention and Sheriff Turner's firm handling of the situation, the memory of Edward's unhinged face and the terror at that moment lingered. The bell above the door chimed again, and Maggie looked up, shaking herself from her thoughts. Her heart lifted slightly when she saw Daniel Whitaker step inside, his familiar frame calming her racing thoughts. He had been steady in the chaos, always there when she needed him most.

"Maggie," Daniel greeted softly, his voice filled with warmth and concern as he approached the counter. "How are you holding up?"

Maggie sighed, her fingers brushing nervously over the ledger.

"I'm... better, I guess. Just trying to get back to normal."

She paused, her eyes meeting his.

"But I can't stop thinking about what happened. It's hard to believe it's over."

Daniel leaned on the counter, his hazel eyes filled with quiet understanding.

"It's normal to feel that way after something like that. You don't have to pretend you're fine, Maggie. What happened was serious."

His words, spoken with such calm sincerity, caused a lump to form in her throat. She swallowed hard, forcing herself to keep it together.

"I was so scared, Daniel. I didn't think… I didn't think it would ever get to that point." Daniel's expression softened, and he reached across the counter, gently placing his hand over hers. The touch was reassuring and grounding.

"You don't have to face this alone. I'm here. Clara's here. You've got people who care about you, Maggie."

For a moment, Maggie didn't know what to say. The warmth of Daniel's hand on hers and the steady look in his eyes was all so comforting. But the moment's vulnerability made her feel exposed in a way she wasn't used to. She had always prided herself on handling things independently, but Daniel was different. He made her feel like it was okay to lean on someone else.

"Thank you," she whispered, her voice barely above a breath. "I don't know what I'd have done without you."

Daniel gently squeezed her hand before pulling back, his eyes never leaving hers.

"You won't have to find out. I'll always be here."

Before either of them could say more, the door swung open again, and Clara breezed in, her face a mixture of worry and relief.

"There you are, Maggie. I was just coming to check on you."

Maggie smiled weakly as Clara approached the counter.

"I'm all right, Clara. Really." Clara gave her a knowing look. "You're trying to be, but I know you. That was terrifying for everyone, but especially for you. And I don't think you've had a moment's peace since it happened."

Maggie let out a shaky breath.

"It's just hard to believe it's finally over."

Clara's expression softened, and she leaned in, her voice gentle but insistent.

"You did the right thing, Maggie. Standing up to him, pressing charges—it took guts. Don't let anyone make you feel otherwise."

Maggie nodded, but Clara's words didn't erase the lingering doubt. Clara glanced at Daniel and then back to Maggie with a more serious look as if reading her mind.

"And don't think this changes who you are for a second. You're still the strongest, most capable person I know. You need time to process all this."

Maggie opened her mouth to respond, but the door creaked open again just then, and Sheriff Amos Turner walked in. His tall frame and no-nonsense demeanor immediately drew the attention of the room. His leather duster still smelled faintly of the outdoors, and his gray eyes held the same quiet authority that had made him a respected figure in Briarwood for years.

"Good afternoon, Miss Hartwell, Mr. Whitaker," the sheriff said, nodding to both of them before stepping further into the store. "I wanted to check in and give you an update on the situation with Edward Townsend."

Maggie's heart skipped a beat. Despite knowing Edward was locked away, the very mention of his name made her stomach twist.

"Is he still in jail?" she asked quietly.

Sheriff Turner's expression remained stoic, but there was a gentleness in his tone as he spoke.

"He's still in custody, yes. But I won't lie to you, Maggie—his family isn't taking this lightly. They're already making noise about getting him out on bail. His father has some influence, and I wouldn't be surprised if they try to pull a few strings."

Maggie's chest tightened at the thought. She hadn't even considered what would happen if Edward was released.

"What does that mean for me?" she asked, her voice quieter now.

The sheriff's gaze softened. "It means we need to stay vigilant. If he does get out, you'll be the first to know, and we'll make sure you're protected. I'm not taking any chances with your safety."

Daniel, who had remained quiet, stepped forward, his tone serious.

"If Edward tries anything, he'll have more than the sheriff to deal with."

Sheriff Turner nodded in agreement.

"We're keeping a close eye on him, don't you worry. But it's important that you come by later to formalize the complaint. We'll need everything in writing."

Maggie swallowed hard, nodding. "I'll come by."

With a respectful tip of his hat, the sheriff turned to leave.

"You take care of yourself, Miss Hartwell. And don't hesitate to reach out if anything feels off."

As the door closed behind him, the weight of everything settled heavily over Maggie. Clara gave her a supportive smile.

"You'll be all right, Mags. You've got us."

Maggie looked between Clara and Daniel, her heart swelling with gratitude for the people who stood by her. Despite the fear and uncertainty, she realized she wasn't alone in this battle. For the first time in a long while, she felt like she could lean on others without feeling weak.

"Thank you," she said again, her voice firmer this time. "I mean it."

Daniel nodded, his gaze softening.

"Anytime."

As the day wore on and the sun began to set, Daniel offered to help Maggie close up the shop. The conversation drifted to lighter topics as they worked, but the tension between them—the unspoken connection—hung in the air. By the time they finished, the store was quiet, the dimming light casting a soft glow through the windows.

"I'll walk you home," Daniel offered, his voice gentle.

Maggie hesitated for a moment, but then nodded, feeling the warmth of his presence beside her as they stepped out into the cool evening air. The walk was quiet, the night calm after the chaos of the past few days. When they reached Maggie's front door, she turned to face him, her heart fluttering with a mixture of gratitude and something deeper, something she hadn't quite named yet.

"Daniel, I… I don't know how to thank you enough for everything."

Daniel smiled, the corners of his eyes crinkling with warmth.

"You don't have to thank me, Maggie. I'm just glad you're safe."

For a brief moment, they stood there in the soft glow of the lantern light, the world around them quiet and still. The tension between them was palpable, the unspoken feelings lingering in the air. But before either of them could say more, Maggie smiled softly and stepped back toward the door.

"Goodnight, Daniel," she said, her voice barely a whisper.

"Goodnight, Maggie," Daniel replied, his eyes lingering on her as she disappeared inside. As the door clicked shut, Maggie leaned against it, her heart racing. The storm may not have passed completely, but for now, in this quiet moment, she felt safe.

Chapter Eleven: A New Morning on Whitaker Farm

The first light of dawn spread across the rolling fields of Whitaker Farm, turning the dewy grass a pale gold. The soft chirping of birds filled the air, and the distant sound of cattle lowing could be heard as Daniel Whitaker stepped out of his modest farmhouse. He stood for a moment on the wide porch, breathing in the fresh morning air and looking out over the land he'd worked for years. The farm stretched as far as the eye could see, with rows of cornfields to one side and pastures filled with grazing cattle to the other. Behind the house, a small orchard stood proudly, with the apple trees bearing fruit. Beyond that, a winding creek cut through the land, providing fresh water for the crops and livestock.

The land had been in his family for generations, and though it was hard work, Daniel wouldn't trade this life for anything. He wiped the last traces of sleep from his eyes and stretched his broad shoulders, mentally preparing himself for the long day ahead. Running a farm this size required an early start, and Daniel always made sure he was the first one out. But he didn't run it alone—he had a team of farmhands who had become like family to him over the years.

The first to arrive was Sam Jenkins, a wiry man in his early forties who had worked on the Whitaker farm since Daniel's father had run things. Sam was dependable, always quick with a joke, but never afraid of hard work. His thin, weathered face broke into a grin as he approached Daniel.

"Mornin', boss," Sam greeted, tipping his hat. "We're in for a good day today. Got the weather on our side, at least."

Daniel nodded, smiling slightly.

"Let's hope it stays that way. The cornfields are lookin' good, but we need to keep a close eye on the herd today. I've got a feeling one of the cows is close to calving." Sam chuckled, slapping his hat against his thigh.

"You and those cows, Whitaker. You've got a sense for 'em, that's for sure."

Not long after Sam, Hank Wilkins appeared, a hulking man in his early thirties working on the farm for several years. Hank didn't say much, but his strength and skill with the animals made him indispensable. He nodded at Daniel as he approached, his face calm and steady as ever.

"Got the fence fixed in the north field," Hank said in his low, gravelly voice. "We'll be good to move the cattle in there later."

"Good work, Hank," Daniel replied. "Let's make sure everything's set before we start the harvest later."

The final member of the team, Pete McAllister, arrived shortly after, bringing a bundle of energy with him. Younger than the others, Pete was in his twenties and had grown up nearby, eager to prove himself as a farmhand. His blond hair was always a little too long, falling into his eyes as he worked, but his enthusiasm more than made up for it.

"Morning, Mr. Whitaker!" Pete called out, bounding toward the barn. "Ready for another day?"

Daniel nodded, appreciating Pete's energy, though he sometimes worried the young man didn't pace himself.

"Let's not rush it, Pete. Got a long day ahead of us."

The four men fell into their familiar routine, tending to the animals and checking on the fields. The farm was a well-oiled machine that required constant attention to keep things running smoothly.

As the sun rose higher in the sky, Daniel found himself thinking of Maggie. He hadn't seen her since the evening he'd walked her home, and though he knew she was busy recovering from the events at the festival, he couldn't help but wonder how she was doing. The thought of her always brought warmth and protectiveness, especially now that he knew she was still grappling with what had happened with Edward.

"Boss?" Sam's voice interrupted his thoughts, and Daniel blinked, realizing he'd been staring at the fields without seeing them.

"Yeah, Sam?" Daniel asked, turning to his farmhand.

Sam gave him a knowing look.

"You thinkin' about that girl from the store again?"

Daniel frowned slightly, though a faint smile tugged at the corner of his mouth.

"What makes you say that?"

Sam chuckled. "The way you've been starin' off like that, it's a dead giveaway. Don't worry, though. I reckon she's thinkin' about you too."

Before Daniel could respond, the sound of a horse's hooves approaching caught their attention. Daniel turned toward the road leading up to the farm and saw two figures on horseback riding toward the house.

As they drew closer, he recognized Maggie and Clara, their horses trotting gracefully up the dirt path.

"Speak of the devil," Sam muttered with a grin, tipping his hat toward the ladies as they approached.

Maggie dismounted gracefully, her cheeks flushed from the ride. Daniel's heart gave a little flutter as she smiled at him, her face lighting up the way it always did. Clara followed suit, her usual playful expression in place as she caught Daniel's eye.

"Good morning, gentlemen," Clara said, her voice teasing as she glanced between Daniel and Maggie. "We thought we'd pay a visit and see what kind of hard work you all are up to." Daniel chuckled, walking over to meet them.

"Mornin', ladies. Didn't expect to see you out here today."

Maggie smiled softly, her eyes meeting Daniel's.

"We figured we could use a change of scenery. Plus, Clara's been wanting to see your farm." Clara grinned, taking in the wide fields and the neat rows of crops. "And I must say, Daniel, you run a fine operation here. It's beautiful."

Daniel felt a sense of pride swell in his chest as he looked over the land. "Thank you, Clara. It's a lot of work, but I wouldn't trade it for anything."

Maggie's eyes softened as she looked around, clearly impressed by the farm's vastness and the care Daniel put into it.

"It's peaceful here," she said quietly, her gaze drifting to the grazing cattle in the distance.

Daniel nodded, feeling a sense of contentment in Maggie's approval.

"That's why I love it. It's hard work, but it's honest work." Pete, ever eager, came bounding over from the barn, his eyes wide with excitement at seeing the women.

"Good morning, Miss Hartwell! Good morning, Miss Adams! You should see the cornfields—we've got the best crop this season!"

Maggie laughed softly, amused by Pete's enthusiasm.

"I'm sure it's wonderful, Pete. You all must work hard to keep this place running."

Daniel watched as the farmhands introduced themselves to Clara and Maggie, each one clearly taken by the visitors. Sam leaned in to whisper something to Hank, who gave a rare, quiet chuckle. Even stoic Hank seemed more animated in their presence.

The farm had never felt quite so alive, and as Daniel stood there with Maggie and Clara, he couldn't help but feel that things were changing—slowly, but surely. This visit was a reminder that life on the farm while fulfilling, was about more than just the land. It was about the people he shared it with.

Chapter Twelve: A Picnic for Two

The sun was high in the sky, casting a soft, golden glow over the fields of Whitaker Farm. The warm breeze carried the scent of fresh grass and blooming flowers, and the sound of the creek's gentle babbling filled the air as Daniel led Maggie down a narrow path that wound through the orchard. "This way," Daniel said, his voice soft and easy as he guided her toward his favorite spot on the farm. Maggie followed him, her heart light and her steps steady as they made their way to the creek.

She had been to the farm several times now, but this part of the land—quiet, secluded—was new to her. The towering oak trees provided shade, and the sunlight filtered through the leaves, creating a dappled pattern on the ground. Finally, they reached a small clearing by the creek, where Daniel had already laid out a blanket under one of the oak trees. The sound of the water trickling gently over the smooth stones added to the peacefulness of the scene.

"This is beautiful," Maggie said, her voice full of quiet awe as she entered the setting.

Daniel smiled, pleased that she liked it.

"I thought you might appreciate a break from the shop, some fresh air."

He gestured to the blanket where a basket sat waiting.

"And some good food, of course."

Maggie smiled as she sat on the blanket, smoothing her skirt beneath her. Daniel joined her, opening the basket and pulling out the picnic spread he had carefully prepared. There were slices of fresh bread, still warm from the oven, a jar of homemade strawberry preserves, blocks of cheese, and a bundle of grapes from the vineyard down the road. A small bottle of lemonade sat nestled in the basket, and there were even a few slices of pie—still warm from the farm's kitchen.

"You went all out," Maggie said with a teasing smile as she took in the spread.

Daniel chuckled, a hint of shyness in his voice.

"I figured if I was going to take you on a picnic, I might as well do it right."

They began to eat, the simple yet delicious meal filling the quiet space between them. The bread was soft and buttery, the preserves sweet and tangy, and the cheese sharp and flavorful. As they ate, the conversation flowed easily, much like the creek beside them.

Daniel told Maggie about the farm's history, how his family had settled there generations ago, and how much it meant to him to keep the land thriving. Maggie listened, captivated by his connection to the place, admiring the quiet pride that filled his voice.

"You must feel so rooted here," Maggie said softly, her eyes drifting over the fields stretching beyond the trees.

Daniel nodded, his gaze thoughtful.

"It's home, always has been. I can't imagine being anywhere else."

Maggie smiled, feeling a warmth spread through her chest. She admired how grounded Daniel was and how tied he was to the land and his family's legacy. It contrasted the uncertainty she had felt in her life lately, especially with Edward's threats still looming in the back of her mind.

"I envy that," Maggie admitted after a moment. "The way you've built your life here. It must be… comforting."

Daniel glanced at her, his hazel eyes soft.

You've built something, too, Maggie. The store, your town life—you're just as strong as any farmer. Don't sell yourself short."

His words settled over her like a balm, and for a moment, the lingering tension she'd been carrying since the festival seemed to ease. She looked at him, their eyes meeting, and felt that familiar flutter in her chest—the one she couldn't quite name but that was growing stronger with every passing day.

As they sat together, the sun beginning its slow descent toward the horizon, Daniel reached for the bottle of lemonade, their hands brushing briefly. The simple touch sent a spark through Maggie, her pulse quickening in response. Daniel seemed to notice it too, though he said nothing, only offering her a small smile as he poured the lemonade into two glasses. The peacefulness of the afternoon wrapped around them, and for a brief, perfect moment, the world outside the farm seemed to disappear. It was just the two of them, sharing this quiet space, the unspoken connection between them deepening with every passing second. As they finished their meal, the sound of hooves approaching broke the stillness, and both Maggie and Daniel turned to see Clara riding toward them on her horse. Her face was alight with amusement as she pulled up beside the picnic site.

"Well, well," Clara teased as she dismounted, giving Maggie a playful grin. "It looks like someone's been enjoying a lovely afternoon."

Maggie laughed softly, shaking her head. "You couldn't resist, could you?"

Clara shrugged, her eyes twinkling.

"I was curious. And besides, someone had to check on you two. Make sure you weren't getting into too much trouble."

Daniel chuckled, standing up to greet Clara.

"Trouble? I'm not sure Maggie and I are the troublemaking type."

Clara raised an eyebrow, still grinning.

"Maybe not, but I wouldn't put it past you, Daniel."

The lighthearted banter continued as Clara joined them, sitting on the blanket and eyeing the remains of their picnic.

"I see you've brought out the best of the farm, Daniel. I'm impressed."

"It's nothing too fancy," Daniel replied modestly. "Just something simple."

Clara gave Maggie a knowing look.

"I don't know, I think it's pretty impressive." Maggie blushed slightly, brushing her hair behind her ear. "It was a perfect picnic."

The three of them chatted for a while longer, the sun dipping lower in the sky, casting a warm, golden light over the fields. The farm's peacefulness and companionship of Clara and Daniel felt like a balm to Maggie's frayed nerves, a reminder that despite the challenges she'd faced, there was still good in the world. There was still peace to be found. After a while, Clara stood, stretching and giving Maggie a wink.

"I think I'll leave you two to enjoy the sunset. I've got to head back into town anyway." Maggie rolled her eyes, though a smile played on her lips.

"You're impossible." Clara winked at Daniel, who smiled good-naturedly as she mounted her horse.

"Take care, Maggie. I'll see you soon."

As Clara rode off into the distance, Maggie and Daniel were left alone again, the warm glow of the setting sun casting a golden hue over the farm. The air between them felt charged, the moment's quiet full of unspoken things. Daniel turned to face Maggie, his eyes soft as he spoke.

"I'm glad you came today."

Maggie smiled, her heart feeling lighter than it had in days.

"So am I."

They sat in the fading light, their connection growing stronger with each passing moment, the world around them fading into the background as they shared this perfect, peaceful evening together.

Chapter Thirteen: Unsettling News

The morning sunlight filtered through the windows of Hartwell Mercantile as Maggie absently wiped down the counter, trying to distract herself from the growing unease in her chest. It had been a few days since Edward was locked away, and she had hoped that would end. But deep down, she knew it wouldn't be that simple. The bell above the door jingled, and Maggie glanced up to see Sheriff Turner stepping inside. His face was grim, and Maggie's heart sank instantly.

"Maggie," the sheriff said in his usual calm, measured tone, but the look in his eyes was enough to tell her what was coming. "I've got some news. Edward's been released."

Her heart skipped a beat.

"Released? How?" Sheriff Turner sighed, his lips tightening. "His family pulled some strings. They've got influence in the county, more than I'd like to admit. The judge allowed him to go free on what they're calling 'good behavior' and promises from his family. There's not much more I can do for now."

Maggie's stomach twisted. She had known Edward's family held sway in the area, but she hadn't expected them to move so quickly or easily.

"So, he's free to do whatever he wants?"

The sheriff shook his head.

"Not entirely. He's been warned to stay away from you, and I'll watch him closely. But I wanted to let you know so you can stay cautious."

Maggie nodded, though the anxiety was already creeping in. Edward wasn't the kind of man to take warnings seriously, and the thought of him being free again filled her with dread.

"Thank you, Sheriff," she said quietly. "I'll be careful."

The sheriff gave her a sympathetic look before tipping his hat and leaving. As the door closed behind him, Maggie felt the weight of Edward's release pressing down on her. She had tried to move on and find peace, but it seemed like Edward's influence—like his family's power—would always find a way to pull her back into his orbit.

Later that day, Maggie makes her way to Whitaker Farm, needing to share the news with Daniel. As she walked through the fields, her mind raced with thoughts of Edward and what might come next. Daniel was working near the barn when she arrived, tending to the cattle. His broad shoulders moved easily as he worked, and seeing him brought a small measure of comfort to Maggie's troubled thoughts. She approached him slowly, her footsteps soft in the dirt.

"Daniel," she called out.

He turned at the sound of her voice, his expression immediately softening when he saw her.

"Maggie. Everything all right?"

Maggie shook her head, her voice barely above a whisper.

"Edward's been released." Daniel's jaw tightened, and for a moment, his hazel eyes darkened with anger.

"How?" he asked, though Maggie could tell he already knew the answer. "His family," she replied, her voice tinged with frustration. "They pulled strings. He's out, and there's nothing more the sheriff can do."

Daniel stepped toward her, his gaze hard.

"He's not going to come near you, Maggie. I won't let that happen."

Maggie smiled weakly, grateful for his unwavering support.

"Thank you, Daniel. I know I shouldn't worry, but… I can't help it. Whenever I think it's over, he finds a way back."

Daniel's eyes softened as he placed a hand gently on her shoulder.

"You don't have to face this alone. You know that, right?"

Maggie nodded, though her heart still felt heavy.

"It just feels like no matter what I do, his family will always have the upper hand." Daniel's voice was firm, filled with quiet determination.

"Not this time, Maggie. He might have influence, but that doesn't mean he's untouchable. And he won't get anywhere near you as long as I'm around."

They stood there for a moment, the air thick with unspoken words. The warmth of Daniel's hand on her shoulder was comforting, and Maggie felt a flicker of something stronger than fear—something she couldn't quite name but was growing with every passing day.

As the tension between Maggie and Daniel lingered in the air, the sound of footsteps approached from the other side of the barn. Pete McAllister appeared, wiping sweat from his brow, his expression brightening when he saw Maggie.

"Well, if it isn't the best company in town," Pete said with a grin, his eyes darting briefly to Clara, who was trailing not far behind him.

It didn't take much to see that Pete had taken a particular interest in Clara, and today was no exception. Clara, ever the sharp-witted one, raised an eyebrow at Pete's remark.

"You're laying it on thick today, aren't you, Pete?" Pete laughed, his usual enthusiasm shining through. "What can I say? A good day's work and good company—it's all a man could ask for."

Clara smirked, glancing at Maggie.

"I think we've got ourselves a charmer."

Maggie couldn't help but smile at the playful exchange. Pete's obvious affection for Clara had become more apparent with each passing visit, and though

Clara often played it cool, there was a softness in her eyes whenever Pete was around.

"Careful, Pete," Maggie teased lightly. "Clara doesn't fall for smooth talk that easily."

Pete grinned, undeterred. "I'm up for the challenge."

The banter brought a welcome lightness to the otherwise tense day, and for a few moments, Maggie allowed herself to laugh, the weight of Edward's release momentarily lifting.

The news of Edward's release spread through town as the afternoon wore on. When Maggie returned to the shop later that day, she heard whispers from a few customers near the counter.

"I heard Edward Townsend's back," one woman said quietly, glancing toward the door as if expecting him to walk in at any moment.

"He's dangerous," another replied.

"That family's got too much power. It's no wonder he's out."

Maggie's heart sank as she listened to the hushed conversations. The town had already begun to speculate, and the pressure was mounting. Some townsfolk supported her decision to stand up to Edward, while others whispered about how his family's influence could make her life difficult.

As she returned to her work, Maggie couldn't help but feel the weight of the town's eyes on her. But despite the fear and uncertainty, she knew one thing for sure: she wasn't facing this alone.

Chapter Fourteen: A New Chapter at the Store

The next morning, the first rays of sunlight crept through the farmhouse window as Maggie rose from the bed. She stretched, feeling exhaustion from the previous day and relief that today would be different. She saddled Willow for her ride into town, Bear trailing behind her. As the morning air filled her lungs, calm settled over her. Today, she wouldn't be alone in the store.

When Maggie arrived at Hartwell Mercantile, Clara was already standing at the door, a basket of baked goods from her kitchen in her arms, her smile as bright as ever.

"Mornin', Maggie," Clara called out, her voice full of cheer. "Ready to tackle the day?"

Maggie smiled back, the weight of yesterday's events lightening with Clara's presence.

"I'm glad you're here, Clara. It feels… better with you around." Clara winked, opening the door to the store.

"Of course it does! I'll scare off any troublemakers with my charm alone."

Maggie couldn't help but laugh, and the sound felt like relief after everything that had happened. Together, they opened the store, arranging the goods on the shelves, the rhythm of their teamwork falling into place naturally. Clara, ever the efficient one, organized the counter with precision while Maggie restocked the pantry shelves. As they worked, Clara's lively chatter filled the air, keeping the mood light and fun. She recounted a humorous story about one of the local farmers nearly tripping over his boots while trying to impress his wife with a new plow, her laughter contagious as she added her usual flair to the tale.

"Honestly, Maggie," Clara said with a chuckle as she adjusted a display of freshly delivered goods, "if I had half the luck that man's wife does, I'd be twice as rich by now."

Maggie shook her head, smiling.

"I think you'd manage just fine without a farmer to keep you afloat."

Clara flashed a mischievous grin.

"Maybe, but it wouldn't hurt to have a little help now and then."

Their conversation drifted naturally between work and gossip, with Clara occasionally poking fun at some of the customers they both knew so well. The way Clara moved about the store, making sure everything was in its place and that the customers felt welcome, helped ease Maggie's mind, making the store feel like the safe haven it had once been before Edward's presence darkened its doors.

"I tell you what," Clara said, wiping her hands on her apron as she turned to Maggie, "this place has always had charm, but with the two of us running it? It'll be the finest mercantile in Missouri."

Maggie raised an eyebrow, smirking at her friend's confidence.

"Is that so? Should I be worried you'll take over the place?"

Clara leaned against the counter, her eyes twinkling.

"Oh, Maggie. I've got enough on my plate without stealing your livelihood, but I do enjoy being here with you. This feels… right."

Maggie's smile softened, her heart warming at Clara's words.

"It feels right to me, too. I didn't realize how much I needed this—how much I needed you."

Clara's face softened in return.

"That's what friends are for. We'll get through this, Maggie, and when it's all said and done, we'll laugh about it over a bottle of wine."

As they continued working through the day, Clara's sharp eye didn't miss a thing. She helped customers with the kind of ease that made them feel like old friends, all while sharing little jokes with Maggie. Even the most mundane task seemed to take on a lighthearted quality with Clara by her side. In the early afternoon, Clara paused to stretch and glanced at Maggie.

"You know, this store really could use a little sprucing up. Maybe add some curtains to the windows or bring in a few more plants."

Maggie laughed, raising an eyebrow. "Curtains? Plants? Are we turning the store into a home now?"

Clara grinned, unfazed. "Why not? People are drawn to things that feel warm and welcoming. Trust me, curtains are the answer."

Maggie shook her head, amused by her friend's endless ideas. "If it'll make you happy, we'll add curtains."

"I'll hold you to that," Clara said with a playful wink, making a mental note to find some fabric for the new addition.

As the day wore on, Maggie realized how much easier everything felt with Clara. The weight of the fear that had gripped her since Edward's attack had begun to lift, and for the first time in days, Maggie felt like things were returning to normal—or at least something close to it.

That evening, as Maggie rode Willow back to Whitaker Farm, she found herself looking forward to the quiet of the countryside. The sun was low in the sky, casting a warm golden light over the fields, and the rhythmic clip-clop of Willow's hooves was a soothing contrast to the bustle of the store. When she arrived, Daniel was there to greet her once again. This time, though, there was something different in the way his eyes lingered on her as she dismounted. The connection between them, unspoken but undeniable, seemed to have grown stronger with each passing day.

"How was the store?" Daniel asked, his voice soft as he reached to help her down. Maggie smiled, feeling a warmth in her chest.

"Clara's been a godsend. It's like she knows how to make everything feel lighter."

Daniel nodded, his eyes softening as he listened.

"I'm glad you've got her with you. You deserve to have someone by your side."

Maggie glanced at him, her heart fluttering at the sincerity in his voice. "I'm lucky," she admitted softly, though part of her knew she wasn't just talking about Clara. With Daniel nearby, the lingering fear of Edward's return didn't seem overwhelming. In fact, with Daniel, Maggie felt safer than she ever had. As they walked toward the house, Bear bounded toward them, his tail wagging as he circled Maggie in excitement. Maggie laughed, reaching down to pat him as she looked back at Daniel.

"He's always happy to see me." Daniel smiled.

"Smart dog."

They continued inside, the warmth of the farmhouse wrapping around Maggie as they settled in for dinner. As always, Daniel had ensured everything was perfect—roasted vegetables, warm bread, and a stew that filled the air with the most comforting aromas.

"Honestly," Maggie said as she sat down, "you've outdone yourself again."

Daniel chuckled, his eyes twinkling as he poured them each a glass of lemonade.

"It's nothing fancy. Just making sure you're taken care of."

Maggie smiled, her heart swelling with gratitude. In the quiet of the evening, with the fire crackling in the hearth and Bear resting at her feet, she couldn't help but feel like, despite everything, life was slowly starting to fall into place. And with Daniel's steady presence beside her, that peace felt more possible than ever before.

Chapter Fifteen: Storm on the Horizon

The morning began like any other, with a soft, golden light filtering through the windows of Whitaker Farm. But something felt off, even as Maggie stepped outside to check on Willow and Bear. The air was unusually still, and a heaviness clung to the atmosphere. Dark clouds had begun gathering on the horizon, swirling like a storm brewing just beyond the hills. Daniel stood near the barn, his gaze fixed on the sky. His brow furrowed as he watched the dark clouds rolling in, and he could feel the change in the air—a farmer's instinct honed by years of working the land.

"Good Mornin', Maggie," he greeted, his voice low, eyes still on the horizon.

Maggie approached him; concern etched on her face.

"It feels… strange today."

Daniel nodded, turning toward her with a serious expression.

"Storm's coming. A bad one."

The wind began to pick up, swirling dust around their feet. Maggie shivered despite the warmth of the day, sensing the weight of his words.

"How bad do you think?"

"Hard to say," Daniel said, his voice thoughtful, eyes scanning the sky. "But we need to be ready. These storms don't give much warning. We need to tie everything down and shelter the animals. There's no telling how long it'll last."

By mid-morning, the wind had become fierce, howling through the trees and bending the tall grass as Maggie and Daniel rushed to secure the farm. Hank, along with Sam and Pete, was already hard at work, helping to move the livestock into the barn and secure anything that could be blown away. Hank, ever the stoic presence, worked silently but efficiently, his strong frame comforting as he wrestled with the barn doors, ensuring they were latched tightly. He glanced at Daniel, who was nearby, helping Maggie secure the toolshed.

"This one's comin' fast," Hank said in his low, gravelly voice. "We'd better get everything inside quick. Won't take long for it to hit us hard."

Daniel nodded, his eyes sharp with focus.

"You're right. We'll move as fast as we can. Once the animals are secure, everyone needs to take shelter."

Maggie and Daniel saddled their horse to set off toward Briarwood as the storm bore down. The wind howled louder with each passing minute, and the sky had darkened to an ominous gray, flashing with streaks of lightning. When they reached Hartwell Mercantile, Clara was already standing in the doorway, her face pale and drenched with rain.

Maggie hurried toward her, calling out over the wind, "Clara!"

Together, the three worked quickly to bring in the last of the goods from outside, battling the fierce gusts that tried to throw them off balance. Maggie, Clara, and Daniel barely managed to secure the windows and shutters before the storm hit with full force. The storm roared over Briarwood, battering the town with rain and wind that seemed to tear at the very foundation of the buildings. The three of them huddled inside the store, eyes wide as the noise outside grew deafening.

Trees bent under the wind, and splintering wood echoed through the air. Suddenly, there was a loud crash outside, and Clara gasped.

"What was that?" "I'll check it out," Daniel said, already heading for the door.

As Daniel disappeared into the storm, Maggie and Clara stayed behind, anxiety gripping them both. A few moments later, Daniel returned, rain-soaked but unharmed.

"One of the trees in the square came down," he explained, shaking water from his hair. "It took out part of the fence, but no one's hurt."

Maggie let out a sigh of relief, though her heart still raced with worry. When the storm finally began to subside, Daniel, Maggie, and Clara ventured outside to assess the damage. The streets of Briarwood were littered with debris—fallen branches, shattered fences, and scattered belongings from the shops. The air, heavy with moisture, still carried the scent of rain, but the worst had passed.

"We need to check on the farm," Daniel said, his tone urgent but calm. "The animals… we need to see if they're all right."

Maggie's heart clenched at the thought of Bear, and together, they made their way back toward Whitaker Farm, navigating the debris-strewn roads as quickly as possible. When they arrived, they were greeted by a reassuring sight—Bear came bounding toward them, unscathed by the storm, his tail wagging furiously. In the barn, the animals were accounted for, thanks to the efforts of Hank, Sam, and Pete. Hank, who had been checking the structure of the barn for any damage, walked over to Daniel.

"We got lucky. No major damage, just a few fence posts down."

Daniel nodded, his eyes scanning the area.

"Good work, Hank. Let's get the fence repaired as soon as we can."

The next day, with the storm finally behind them, the residents of Briarwood came together to rebuild. Hank, ever the dependable farmhand, worked alongside Sam and Pete to restore Whitaker Farm's fences and clear the debris scattered across the fields. His strong, silent presence was a comforting reminder of the community's resilience.

Over in town, Maggie and Clara set about cleaning up the store, sweeping up broken glass, and rearranging the goods the storm had tossed about. Clara made light of the situation as they worked, her usual playful demeanor a welcome distraction from the overwhelming recovery task.

"You know, Maggie," Clara said with a smirk, "I think this storm was the town's way of telling us it's time to redecorate."

Maggie laughed, shaking her head.

"I think I've had enough excitement for one day, Clara. Let's focus on getting things back to normal."

Together, with the help of the townspeople, the fences were mended, the streets cleared, and the town slowly began to return to its former self. The storm had brought chaos but also brought the community together in a way that reminded them of their strength and resilience.

As the sun set on another long day of repairs, Maggie stood on the porch of Whitaker Farm, watching the sky turn from a deep orange to the soft purples of twilight. Daniel stood beside her, his hand resting lightly on her shoulder. Hank, Sam, and Pete were still working in the distance, their silhouettes moving steadily against the fading light.

"We made it through," Maggie said softly, her voice filled with gratitude.

Daniel nodded, his gaze fixed on the horizon.

"We always will."

And in that moment, surrounded by the quiet peace of the farm, Maggie knew that no matter what storms lay ahead—whether they came from the sky or the challenges in her life—she wouldn't face them alone.

Chapter Sixteen: New Days Ahead

The days after the storm were filled with the steady rhythm of recovery. Briarwood buzzed with the sound of hammers, saws, and the chatter of townsfolk coming together to repair the damage left behind. The once chaotic streets had returned to normal, though the scars of the storm still lingered in the broken fences and the occasional toppled tree. For Maggie, the work at Hartwell Mercantile kept her busy, but it was the quiet moments at Whitaker Farm that felt most grounding. Every evening, after a long day of mending the store with Clara, she would ride Willow back to the farm, where Daniel was always there, waiting for her.

One evening, as she rode up the familiar path, Maggie spotted Daniel and Hank working on the barn. The storm had caused more damage than they initially realized, and now Daniel intended to reinforce the structure. Sam and Pete were busy nearby, stacking wood for repairs. Maggie dismounted and made her way over to them, her heart warming at the sight of Daniel, his brow furrowed in concentration as he worked.

"Need a hand?" Maggie asked, her voice light but sincere.

Daniel looked up, wiping the sweat from his brow. His face softened when he saw her, a smile tugging at the corners of his lips.

"I wouldn't say no to an extra pair of hands." Maggie smiled and joined him, rolling up her sleeves.

For the next hour, they worked side by side, securing the barn walls and reinforcing the roof. Though the task was demanding, the presence of Hank, Sam, and Pete and the occasional lighthearted joke kept the mood light. Hank, ever the quiet one, was focused on the task, but Pete—true to form—couldn't resist stealing glances at Clara, who had arrived not long after Maggie to check on the progress.

"You know," Pete said, trying to sound casual as he stacked the last of the wood, "I've been thinkin' we ought to celebrate once this barn is fixed up. Maybe a little dance in town? What do you think, Clara?"

Clara raised an eyebrow, giving Pete a sly smile.

"A dance, you say? I didn't take you for the dancing type, Pete."

Pete chuckled, his face reddening slightly.

"Oh, I've got a few moves. You'll just have to come and see for yourself."

Maggie couldn't help but laugh, watching Clara and Pete banter. There was a growing spark between them, and Clara's teasing only seemed to encourage Pete's earnest attempts to win her over.

A few days later, the townsfolk began to organize a small gathering to lift spirits after the storm. The idea had started as a simple community meeting, but it quickly grew into something more—a way for everyone to come together, celebrate their resilience, and enjoy a break from the hard work of rebuilding.

"Are you coming to the gathering tomorrow night?" Clara asked Maggie as they worked in the store the next afternoon, dusting off shelves and rearranging the goods. Maggie nodded, though her mind was preoccupied. The rumors about Edward had been swirling again, and though she hadn't seen him since his failed attack, the thought of him returning made her stomach churn.

"Good," Clara continued, breaking into Maggie's thoughts. "And you should wear something nice. Who knows? Maybe Daniel will be there to sweep you off your feet."

Maggie rolled her eyes, though a faint blush crept into her cheeks.

"It's just a town gathering, Clara. Don't go getting any ideas."

"Oh, I've already got ideas," Clara teased, her eyes twinkling. "I see the way he looks at you, and don't try to pretend you don't feel the same. You two are practically made for each other."

Maggie shook her head, though she couldn't deny that the thought of Daniel had been on her mind more and more lately. His quiet strength, his gentle smile, how he made her feel safe—it was becoming harder to ignore their connection.

The evening of the gathering arrived, and the town square was alive with laughter and music. The townsfolk had brought out lanterns to light the square, and tables were set with food—simple but hearty, a mix of home-baked bread, pies, and roasted meats. Children ran around, their laughter echoing through the streets, while the adults gathered in small groups, talking and catching up after days of hard work. Maggie arrived with Clara, both of them dressed in their best, though Clara had insisted on adding a few extra touches to Maggie's appearance—her hair pinned up in soft curls and a pale blue dress that brought out the brightness of her eyes. "You look beautiful," Clara said with a grin as they approached the crowd. Maggie smiled, though she couldn't shake the nervous flutter in her stomach. She wasn't sure if the crowd or the thought of seeing Daniel had her heart racing.

Daniel stood near the square's edge, talking with Sheriff Turner and a few other men. When he saw Maggie, his expression softened, and he excused himself from the conversation, walking toward her with that easy, familiar smile.

"Maggie," he greeted, his eyes lingering on her longer than usual. "You look… beautiful."

Maggie felt her cheeks flush, but she smiled. "Thank you.

It's good to see everyone together like this." Daniel nodded, glancing around the square. "It's been a hard few weeks, but the town's come through stronger."

As the evening wore on, Maggie and Daniel found themselves drifting away from the crowd, walking together along the outskirts of the square. The music and laughter faded into the background as they talked, the unspoken tension between them growing stronger with every step.

"I'm glad you came tonight," Daniel said softly, his voice carrying a warmth that sent a shiver down Maggie's spine. "After everything that's happened… it's good to see you smiling again."

Maggie looked up at him, her heart fluttering in her chest.

"It's been easier with you around. I don't know how I would've gotten through all of this without you."

For a moment, they stood there, the world around them fading as their connection deepened. Maggie felt a pull, a magnetic force drawing her closer to Daniel, and she knew he felt it, too. But just as the moment stretched, the sound of Clara's laughter broke through the air, reminding Maggie of where they were.

"Come on," Daniel said, his voice low and filled with affection. "Let's get back to the others."

Despite the lightheartedness of the evening, the shadow of Edward still lingered in the back of Maggie's mind. Though the town had begun to heal from the storm, there were still whispers about his return. Some said he had left Briarwood for good, while others believed he was lying low, waiting for the right moment to strike again.

Sheriff Turner had been closely monitoring things, but even he couldn't stop the rumors from spreading.

"We'll handle it if he comes back," he had told Daniel earlier that evening.

But Maggie couldn't help but feel a nagging sense of unease.

As the gathering ended, Daniel and Maggie returned to Whitaker Farm. There were still repairs to be made, and the storm had left them with more work than they had anticipated. Hank, Sam, and Pete had been working tirelessly, but parts of the fence still needed mending, and a few of the animals had wandered off during the chaos.

The next morning, Maggie found herself once again working alongside Daniel, this time helping him repair the fence on the north side of the property. As they worked, their conversation flowed easily, the weight of unspoken feelings still hanging in the air.

"You're becoming quite the farmhand," Daniel said with a smile as Maggie handed him another post.

Maggie laughed, brushing a stray hair from her face.

"I think I'm getting the hang of it."

As the day wore on, Maggie realized just how comfortable she had become at the farm. It felt like home, and the future didn't seem so uncertain with Daniel by her side.

Chapter Seventeen: A New Beginning

The soft morning light filtered through the trees, casting a golden hue over the fields of Whitaker Farm. It was the kind of morning that held promise, where everything felt just a little bit brighter, a little bit lighter. For Maggie, it was a welcome change after the lingering tension of the past few weeks. As she made her way across the yard, Willow trotted alongside her. She spotted Daniel near the barn, his sleeves rolled up as he worked with Hank, Sam, and Pete. The sight of him—strong, steady, always there—filled her with a warmth she couldn't describe. It was as if the world had shifted; she could feel it in every quiet glance they shared. Daniel looked up just as she approached, a smile tugging at the corners of his lips. He wiped the sweat from his brow, his hazel eyes locking on hers with that familiar softness.

"Good mornin', Maggie," he greeted, his voice deep and warm. "How's everything at the store?"

Maggie smiled back, her heart fluttering at the sound of his voice.

"Still closed for now. Clara's been busy redecorating, and I have to say, she's outdone herself. You'll barely recognize it."

Daniel chuckled, his gaze lingering on her.

"Knowing Clara, I'm sure it's something special."

There was a brief pause. The air between them charged with something unspoken. Daniel took a step closer, his expression growing more serious, though his eyes never lost their warmth.

"Maggie," he began slowly, his voice lower now, "there's something I've been wanting to say... something I've been holding back."

Maggie's heart skipped a beat. She had known for a while that there was something more between them than friendship. But hearing it in his voice and how his eyes softened when he looked at her made it all the more real.

"What is it, Daniel?" she asked softly, her pulse quickening.

Daniel hesitated for a moment, his hand brushing lightly against hers. The touch sent a spark through her, and she felt herself drawn to him in a way she couldn't explain.

"I've been thinking a lot about us," Daniel continued, his voice filled with quiet intensity. "About how much you mean to me. I care about you, Maggie. More than I've cared about anyone in a long time."

Maggie felt her breath catch in her throat. The words hung in the air between them, heavy with meaning. She could feel the weight of everything they had been through—the storms, the threats, the uncertainty—and yet, in this moment, none of that seemed to matter. Before she could think and second-guess herself, she stepped closer, her heart pounding. And then, without another word, she leaned in, her lips meeting his in a kiss that was soft and tender but filled with all the emotions they had both kept buried for so long.

For a moment, the world seemed to stop. The sounds of the farm faded into the background, the gentle breeze carrying the scent of hay and earth around them. All Maggie could feel was the warmth of Daniel's arms around her, the steady beat of his heart against hers, and the way his lips moved with hers as if they had always belonged together. When they finally pulled apart, both breathless, Daniel rested his forehead against hers, his eyes filled with something deeper than affection.

"Maggie," he whispered, his voice rough with emotion, "I've wanted to do that for a long time."

Maggie smiled, her heart racing, her cheeks flushed.

"So have I."

They stood there for a while longer, wrapped in the quiet of the morning, their bond stronger than ever. It was a moment Maggie knew she would remember forever—a turning point, a new beginning.

When Maggie arrived at Hartwell Mercantile later that day, the store remained closed, but the transformation was almost complete. Clara had worked tirelessly for two days, pouring her heart and soul into every detail of the redesign. And now, as Maggie stepped inside, she was greeted by a space that felt both familiar and entirely new. Gone were the plain, utilitarian walls and shelves. In their place were soft, warm tones—earthy greens and gentle creams—that made the store feel cozy and inviting. New curtains hung in the windows, catching the afternoon light and casting a soft glow over the room. The shelves had been rearranged carefully, and each display was thoughtfully organized to showcase the best of the store's goods. A small seating area near the front, complete with cushioned chairs and a low table, invited customers to linger, stay a while, and enjoy the warmth of the space. Clara stood in the middle of the room, surveying her work with a satisfied smile.

When she saw Maggie walk in, she spread her arms as if to say, "Look what I've done!"

"Well," Clara grinned, "what do you think? Did I outdo myself, or what?"

Maggie couldn't help but laugh, shaking her head in amazement. "Clara… it's beautiful. You've completely transformed the place."

Clara beamed, clearly pleased with herself. "I told you I had a vision. This store has always had potential, Maggie. It just needed a little… sprucing up."

Maggie wandered around the store, touching the new curtains and admiring the displays. It felt more than just a store now—it felt like a place where people could gather and feel at home.

"You've outdone yourself," Maggie said, turning to face Clara. "It's exactly what this place needed."

Clara's grin widened. "I knew you'd love it. And now, with the new look, we can split shifts. You take some days, I'll take others, and we get more time for ourselves."

Maggie nodded, thinking about how much easier it would be to manage everything with Clara taking on more responsibility. "It's perfect. And it'll give me more time at the farm."

Clara winked, her eyes twinkling with mischief. "More time with Daniel, you mean."

Maggie felt her cheeks flush, but she couldn't deny it. The time she spent with Daniel had become the highlight of her days, and now, with the kiss they had shared that morning, everything felt like it was finally falling into place.

That evening, as the sun dipped below the horizon, casting the sky in shades of pink and orange, Maggie found herself sitting on the porch of Whitaker Farm, watching the stars begin to twinkle in the darkening sky. Bear lay at her feet, his soft snores filling the quiet air, while Willow grazed peacefully in the nearby pasture. Daniel appeared beside her, his presence comforting as always. He sat down next to her, their shoulders brushing, and for a moment, they sat in silence, simply enjoying the peace of the evening.

"You know," Daniel said after a while, his voice low and thoughtful, "I never thought I'd find something like this again."

Maggie turned to him, her brow furrowed in curiosity. "Something like what?"

Daniel smiled, his gaze softening as he looked at her. "This. You. A life that feels... whole."

Maggie's heart swelled at his words, her chest tightening with emotion.

"I feel the same way," she admitted softly. "For the first time in a long time, I feel like I'm where I'm meant to be."

Daniel reached over, taking her hand in his, his thumb brushing gently against her skin.

"We've been through a lot, Maggie. But I think... I think we're just getting started."

Maggie smiled, leaning against his shoulder as they watched the last rays of sunlight disappear beyond the hills. She knew there would still be challenges ahead—Edward was still a looming threat, and the future was always uncertain—but at this moment, with Daniel by her side, she felt a sense of peace she hadn't known in years. It was a new beginning, a new chapter. And Maggie was ready for whatever came next.

Chapter Eighteen: Unsettling News

The days in Briarwood had begun to settle into a comforting rhythm. The newly redecorated Hartwell Mercantile had become a hub of activity, with customers flowing in and out, drawn by the inviting atmosphere that Clara had so expertly crafted. Even Maggie, who had initially hesitated about the changes, could see the impact. There was a warmth to the store now, a sense of community that hadn't been there before. And despite the lingering shadow of Edward, she couldn't help but feel a glimmer of hope.

It was a sunny afternoon when Clara arrived for her shift, her usual bright energy filling the room. She breezed through the door, carrying a basket of freshly baked bread and greeted Maggie with a wide smile.

"Smells like Heaven in here," Clara announced, setting the basket on the counter. "You'd think we were running a bakery instead of a mercantile."

Maggie chuckled, wiping her hands on her apron. "You might be onto something. Bread and goods might just be the perfect combination."

Clara grinned. "And that's why we make such a great team."

The two of them exchanged easy banter, but a heaviness lurked beneath Maggie's smile. The note. It had been sitting on the counter when Clara had arrived, and though Maggie hadn't opened it yet, she could feel a cold dread pooling in her stomach. As Clara moved to restock a shelf near the front of the store, Maggie hesitated, then slowly reached for the note. It was folded neatly, almost innocently, but the moment her fingers touched the paper, she knew. She knew it was from Edward.

Her heart pounded as she unfolded the note, eyes scanning the brief, chilling message: "I haven't forgotten you. You'll see me soon. –E"

The words seemed to leap off the page, sending a shiver down Maggie's spine. She swallowed hard, her hands trembling as she clutched the paper. For a moment, the room felt too small, too quiet, and the air around her seemed to thicken with the weight of Edward's presence. Seeing the sudden shift in Maggie's demeanor, Clara frowned and set down the goods she'd been stocking. She walked over to the counter, concern etched across her face.

"Maggie, what's wrong?"

Without a word, Maggie handed Clara the note.

As Clara read it, her expression darkened, her usual light-heartedness replaced by a cold fury. "That bastard," Clara hissed, her eyes flashing with anger. "He's still at it. What's he trying to do, scare you into submission?"

Maggie shook her head, her voice barely above a whisper. "I don't know. But he's not going away, Clara. He's still watching. Waiting."

Clara crumpled the note in her fist, her jaw set in determination. "We're not going to let him get away with this. You need to tell Sheriff Turner. And you need to tell Daniel. He can't keep terrorizing you like this."

Maggie nodded, her mind spinning. She had known Edward wouldn't give up so easily, but seeing the threat in writing—seeing those words from him—made it all too real. She couldn't ignore it anymore.

By the time Maggie returned to Whitaker Farm, the sun had begun to set, casting long shadows across the fields. As she dismounted, Willow greeted her with a soft nicker, but Maggie's thoughts were elsewhere. She clutched the crumpled note in her hand, her heart heavy with Edward's looming threat. As she approached the barn, she spotted Daniel working alongside Hank, Sam, and Pete. They were repairing a section of the fence damaged in the storm, their easy banter filling the air. But when Daniel saw her, his expression immediately shifted from relaxed to concerned.

"Maggie," he called out, wiping his hands on a cloth as he made his way over to her. "What's going on? You look—"

"I got this," Maggie interrupted, handing him the note.

Daniel's face darkened as he read the message, his jaw tightening with anger. He crumpled the paper in his hand, his eyes flashing with protectiveness.

"He's still at it? I thought we'd scared him off for good."

Maggie shook her head, her voice trembling slightly. "He's not giving up, Daniel. I don't know what he wants, but he won't leave me alone."

Daniel pulled her into his arms without a word, holding her close. His embrace was strong and steady, grounding her as the fear threatened to overwhelm her.

"We're not letting him get near you," Daniel murmured, his voice rough with emotion. "I'll talk to Sheriff Turner. There's got to be more we can do."

Later that evening, Sheriff Turner arrived at the farm, his face grim as he looked over the note. His eyes were sharp with concern, and he shook his head as he folded the paper and tucked it into his pocket.

"He's playing games," the sheriff said, his voice low and steady. "But we're not going to let him win. I'll keep patrols close by the farm and the store. I've been hearing whispers about him in the next town over—he's been trying to stay out of sight. But this... this means he's planning something."

Maggie's heart pounded at the sheriff's words. "What should we do?"

"Stay alert," the sheriff replied. "I'll keep digging, but if Edward's planning something, we need to be ready."

Despite the tension surrounding Edward, Hartwell Mercantile continued to thrive. The store had become a bustling hub of activity, with customers lingering longer than ever. The warm, inviting atmosphere that Clara had created seemed to draw people in, offering them a sense of comfort and community that Maggie hadn't realized they needed. Clara, ever the spirited presence, was thriving in her role. She easily ran her shifts, making customers feel welcome and at home. And it wasn't long before Pete started making regular appearances at the store, his easy charm and warm smile becoming a fixture in Clara's days.

One afternoon, as Clara was arranging a new shipment of goods, Pete leaned against the counter, watching her with a playful grin.

"You know, Clara," Pete said, his voice teasing, "you've really transformed this place. It feels… different."

Clara glanced over her shoulder, her lips curving into a smirk.

"Well, it's about time someone shook things up around here, don't you think?"

Pete chuckled, his eyes softening as he looked at her. "You're doing a great job. And, you know, if you ever need help… I'm nearby."

Clara raised an eyebrow, her smile widening. "Help with what, exactly?"

"Anything," Pete said, his grin widening. "Anything that gives me an excuse to be here more often."

Clara rolled her eyes but couldn't suppress the warmth that spread through her chest at his words. Pete had a way of making her laugh, of bringing lightness to even the most stressful days. And though she'd never admit it out loud, she was starting to enjoy his company more than she ever expected.

Later that evening, Maggie returned to the farm, her mind still racing with everything that had happened. The note from Edward, Sheriff Turner's warning, the growing success of the store—it was all a whirlwind, and though Daniel had been nothing but supportive, there was a part of her that felt like she was dragging him into something he didn't deserve to be part of. As they sat together on the porch, the stars twinkling overhead, Maggie finally voiced the thoughts that had been weighing on her mind.

"Daniel... I've been thinking," she began softly, her voice hesitant.

Daniel turned to her, his brow furrowing in concern. "What is it?"

Maggie took a deep breath, her gaze fixed on the horizon. "I don't want to put you in danger. This thing with Edward... it's my problem. I don't want you getting hurt because of me."

Daniel's expression hardened, his voice firm but gentle. "Maggie, this isn't just your problem. You're not alone in this. I care about you, and that means we face this together."

Maggie sighed, her heart heavy with guilt. "But what if something happens to you? I couldn't live with myself if—"

"Stop," Daniel interrupted, his tone soft but resolute. He took her hand in his, squeezing it gently. "You're not going to lose me. We're in this together, no matter what happens."

Maggie looked up at him, her eyes glistening with unshed tears. "I just don't want you to get hurt."

"I won't," Daniel reassured her, his thumb brushing gently over her hand. "And neither will you. I promise."

They sat like that for a long time, wrapped in the quiet of the evening, their hearts beating in sync as the night stretched on. The fear of what lay ahead still loomed over them, but in that moment, surrounded by the warmth of Daniel's embrace, Maggie knew they would face whatever came next—together.

Chapter Nineteen: Shadows Deepen

The next few days passed in a haze of unease, with Edward's threat looming over every moment. Despite the growing tension, Maggie tried to keep her focus on the store and her responsibilities at the farm, but there was no escaping the knot of fear that tightened in her chest whenever she thought of the note. Daniel remained a constant source of strength, never leaving her side for long. His presence was a balm to her frayed nerves, though she could sense the simmering anger in him, his frustration at being unable to do more to keep her safe. Sheriff Turner had kept his word, increasing patrols and staying vigilant, but there was only so much the law could do.

On a quiet afternoon, as Maggie closed up the store, Clara walked in, her usual cheerful demeanor a little more subdued than usual. She had heard the rumors around town—rumors that Edward was still lurking, that his influence wasn't as diminished as they had hoped. The town buzzed with speculation, each whispered word carrying a weight that threatened to crush the fragile peace they had found.

"You've been quiet today," Clara said, breaking the silence as she leaned against the counter. "Are you thinking about… him?"

Maggie sighed, brushing a loose strand of hair behind her ear. "It's hard not to. Every time I think we've moved past it, something pulls me back in."

Clara nodded, her eyes filled with empathy. "He's not going to win, Maggie. We won't let him."

Maggie smiled faintly, grateful for her friend's unwavering support. "I know. But it's hard to shake the feeling that something's coming. Something worse."

That evening, after locking up the store, Maggie returned to Whitaker Farm. The sun was setting, casting long shadows across the fields, and the air had turned crisp with the promise of autumn. The peaceful atmosphere did little to calm her nerves, though. Her thoughts were still tangled with fear, her heart heavy with the weight of Edward's unseen presence. When she arrived at the farm, she found Daniel sitting on the porch, his expression thoughtful as he watched the sunset. He stood as she approached, his eyes softening when he saw her.

"You're home early," Daniel remarked, his voice a soothing balm to her frayed nerves. Maggie managed a small smile.

"Clara insisted I take the afternoon off. I think she could tell I wasn't myself."

Daniel stepped closer, wrapping an arm around her shoulders and pulling her into a comforting embrace.

"You've been carrying too much on your shoulders. You don't have to do this alone, Maggie."

"I know," she whispered, leaning into him. "It's just… it's hard. I can't help but feel like we're waiting for the other shoe to drop. Like Edward's out there, planning something. And I don't know what to do."

Daniel's grip tightened slightly, his protective instincts kicking in. "We'll deal with him. Together. Whatever he's planning, he won't get near you. Not if I have anything to say about it."

Maggie closed her eyes, letting the warmth of Daniel's embrace steady her racing heart. She knew he meant every word, but the uncertainty of what lay ahead still lingered, casting a shadow over their quiet moment.

Later that night, long after the sun had disappeared behind the hills, a knock echoed through the quiet farmhouse. Curled by the fire with Daniel, Maggie immediately tensed at the unexpected sound. Daniel stood quickly, his expression sharp with concern as he moved toward the door.

"Who could that be at this hour?" Maggie asked, her voice tight with unease.

Daniel didn't answer, but as he opened the door, Sheriff Turner stood on the porch, his face grim. The sheriff's presence this late could only mean one thing: more bad news.

"Maggie, Daniel," Sheriff Turner greeted, his tone heavy with the weight of what he was about to say. "I didn't want to disturb you this late, but I thought you should know. We've had another sighting of Edward."

Maggie's heart dropped into her stomach, the fear that had been simmering for days flaring into full-blown terror. "Where?"

"Just outside town," the sheriff replied, his expression tight with frustration. "He's been staying out of sight, but we've had a couple of reports of him near the old mill. I've got a few deputies keeping watch, but… I wanted to make sure you were aware. He's not as far away as we thought."

Daniel's face darkened with anger, his jaw clenching as he processed the information. "Why hasn't he been arrested yet?" "We don't have enough evidence to hold him, not without catching him in the act," Sheriff Turner explained. "But rest assured, we're doing everything we can to track him down."

Maggie's hands trembled slightly as she stood beside Daniel, her mind racing. Edward was closer than she had imagined, lurking on the outskirts of their lives, waiting for the perfect moment to strike. The thought made her feel vulnerable in a way she hadn't felt before.

"I'll keep you updated," the sheriff said, his tone gentle but firm. "But I want you both to stay vigilant. He's unpredictable, and we don't know what he's planning."

Maggie nodded, though the fear in her chest was hard to ignore. Daniel closed the door as the sheriff left, his eyes filled with a quiet determination.

"We're going to get through this," Daniel said, his voice steady despite the tension in the air. "I won't let him hurt you, Maggie. Not ever."

Maggie wanted to believe him, to cling to the strength in his words, but the gnawing fear in the pit of her stomach refused to be silenced.

Later that night, long after Sheriff Turner had left, Maggie found herself standing by the window, staring out into the darkness. The farmhouse was quiet, save for the soft crackle of the fire, and yet her mind refused to settle. Daniel approached her from behind, his presence comforting as always. He placed a hand on her shoulder, his touch gentle but grounding.

"Couldn't sleep?" he asked softly, his voice filled with concern. Maggie shook her head, her eyes still fixed on the inky blackness outside. "I keep thinking about what Sheriff Turner said. Edward's out there, Daniel. He's so close. And I don't know what he wants."

Daniel stepped closer, wrapping his arms around her from behind, his chin resting on her shoulder. "Whatever he's planning, we'll be ready for him. You don't have to face this alone."

Maggie leaned into him, her heart heavy with the weight of her fears. "I'm so tired of being scared," she whispered. "I'm tired of looking over my shoulder, waiting for him to show up."

Daniel pressed a soft kiss to her temple, his voice filled with quiet strength.

"You don't have to be scared anymore, Maggie. I'm here. We're in this together."

For a long time, they stood there in the stillness of the night, wrapped in each other's warmth, the fire casting a soft glow around them. Despite the fear that lingered in the air, there was a sense of peace in Daniel's embrace—a reminder that they would face it together no matter what came next.

And at that moment, as the stars twinkled outside and the world seemed to hold its breath, Maggie believed they would get through this—that love, in all its quiet strength, would be enough to carry them through the darkness.

Chapter Twenty: Shadows of Halloween

The air had turned crisp, carrying the unmistakable scent of autumn. The leaves on the trees had begun transforming, shifting from deep greens to vibrant oranges and yellows, blanketing the ground in a riot of color. There was an undeniable chill in the early morning breeze as Maggie stood at the door of Hartwell Mercantile, watching the townspeople prepare for the upcoming Halloween festival. The festival was an annual tradition in Briarwood, one that brought together the entire community. It was a time for storytelling, games, and lighthearted mischief—a chance to forget about the worries of daily life, if only for a night. Clara, ever the enthusiastic organizer, had thrown herself into the preparations, transforming the store into a festive haven. Pumpkins lined the windowsills, their faces carved with grinning expressions, while stalks of corn were tied in bundles at the entrance, welcoming customers with the spirit of the season. Lanterns hung from the ceiling, casting a soft, flickering light that gave the store a cozy, almost magical atmosphere. Clara, standing on a stool to hang more decorations, glanced over her shoulder and grinned at Maggie.

"Isn't this the best time of year?" she asked, her voice filled with excitement. "The whole town's buzzing, everyone getting ready for the festival. You can feel it in the air!"

Maggie smiled, though her heart wasn't fully in it. She couldn't deny the charm of the season—the beauty of the turning leaves, the way the town seemed to come alive with the preparations—but a shadow hung over her, making it hard to fully embrace the festivities.

The note from Edward, his continued presence lurking on the edge of town, had stolen her peace of mind. Even now, as Clara excitedly draped orange and black garlands across the shelves, Maggie found herself glancing out the window, half-expecting to see Edward's face among the crowd.

"You're quiet today," Clara said, stepping down from the stool and dusting off her hands. "Aren't you excited for tonight? It's going to be the biggest Halloween festival we've ever had. And I heard there's going to be a bonfire in the town square."

Maggie forced a smile, trying to shake the unease that had settled in her chest. "I am excited. It's just…"

Clara's smile faltered as she stepped closer, her voice softening. "It's him, isn't it? Edward." Maggie nodded, her gaze dropping to the floor.

"I just can't shake the feeling that something's coming. Sheriff Turner said he's been spotted near town. What if he tries something tonight? What if he's waiting for the perfect moment?"

Clara placed a hand on Maggie's arm, her expression serious but filled with warmth. "You're not alone, Maggie. We'll all be there tonight—Daniel, Sheriff Turner, me. Edward won't get near you. He's a coward. All he does is lurk in the shadows."

Maggie appreciated Clara's words, but fear clung to her like a second skin. She couldn't ignore the gnawing sensation that Edward was closer than anyone realized.

As the afternoon wore on, the streets of Briarwood began filling with people, each busy with preparations for the evening's festivities. Children ran through the square, laughing as they darted between the vendors setting up stalls for the festival. The smell of roasted chestnuts and spiced cider filled the air, mingling with the earthy scent of fallen leaves. It should have been a joyful time, and in many ways, it was. But for Maggie, the excitement was dulled by the constant undercurrent of anxiety. When Daniel arrived at the store later in the afternoon, he immediately noticed the tension in her expression. His brow furrowed as he approached her, concern evident in his eyes.

"Maggie, what's wrong?" he asked, his voice gentle.

Maggie shook her head, trying to brush off her fears. "It's nothing. Just... the festival. A lot is going on."

Daniel wasn't convinced. He reached out, taking her hand in his, his touch warm and steady.

"You've been on edge for days. Is it because of Edward?"

Maggie sighed, her shoulders slumping slightly. "I keep thinking about the note. It's about how close he's been. I can't help but feel like he's waiting for something. And tonight… there will be so many people. It's the perfect opportunity for him to do something."

Daniel's jaw tightened, his protectiveness flaring to the surface. "If he shows up, we'll deal with him. You won't be alone tonight, Maggie. I'll be with you the whole time. And so will Sheriff Turner. Edward's not going to hurt you."

Maggie nodded, grateful for Daniel's presence, but the worry still gnawed at her. She didn't want to ruin the evening with her fears, but the sense of impending danger was impossible to ignore.

As dusk fell, the town square came alive with the glow of lanterns and music. The bonfire had been lit in the center of the square, its flames crackling and dancing in the cool night air. Vendors lined the streets, selling hot cider, roasted chestnuts, and homemade sweets. Children in makeshift costumes—draped in old sheets as ghosts or wearing painted masks—ran through the crowd, their laughter echoing through the evening. Maggie, dressed in a simple dark cloak to ward off the evening chill, walked beside Daniel as they made their way through the festival. Despite the festive atmosphere, she couldn't shake the feeling that something was wrong. Her eyes darted to every shadow, every unfamiliar face in the crowd, half-expecting to see Edward lurking nearby.

"You need to relax," Daniel said softly, his arm wrapped protectively around her waist. "Look around. Everyone's having a good time. Nothing's going to happen tonight."

Maggie wanted to believe him, to let herself get lost in the warmth of the evening, but the tension in her chest refused to loosen its grip. As they passed the bonfire, she caught sight of Clara, who was entertaining a small group of children with one of her famous ghost stories.

"And then," Clara said, her voice low and dramatic, "the ghostly bride appeared at the top of the hill, her white gown billowing in the wind. They say you can still see her on stormy nights, wandering the fields, searching for her lost love…"

The children gasped, their eyes wide with fear and delight. Maggie smiled faintly at Clara's theatrics, but a figure in the distance quickly pulled her attention away. For a split second, she thought she saw Edward—his dark coat and familiar silhouette—standing at the square's edge, watching her. Her breath caught in her throat, her heart pounding as she froze in place, her eyes fixed on the spot where she thought she had seen him. But just as quickly as he had appeared, the figure was gone, swallowed by the crowd.

"Maggie?" Daniel's voice pulled her back to the present, his hand gently squeezing her arm. "What is it?"

"I... I thought I saw him," Maggie whispered, her voice trembling. "Edward. Over there." Daniel's eyes immediately sharpened, scanning the crowd with a protective intensity. "Where?"

Maggie pointed to the edge of the square, but the figure was gone. "He was right there. I saw him."

Daniel frowned, his jaw tight. "Stay close to me. If he's here, we'll find him."

As the evening wore on, the mood in the town remained light and festive despite Maggie's lingering fear. The fortune-telling booth, set up near the bonfire, drew a small crowd eager to test their fates. Clara, always one for theatrics, had taken it upon herself to perform the fortunes, reading tea leaves and reciting old superstitions with a mischievous glint in her eye.

"Who's next?" Clara called, her voice filled with playful excitement.

A young girl, no older than twelve, stepped forward, her eyes wide with curiosity. Clara grinned and gestured for the girl to sit. She took the girl's hands in hers, her voice dropping to a whisper as she began the fortune. Maggie watched from the sidelines, trying to focus on the lightheartedness of the moment. But her mind kept drifting back to the figure she had seen. Was it really Edward? Or was her mind playing tricks on her? As the night wore on, the festivities began to wind down. The bonfire crackled softly, casting long shadows across the square. The crowd had thinned, and Maggie stood by the fire, staring into the flames, her mind heavy with worry. Daniel stepped up beside her, his presence grounding her.

"You ready to head back?" Maggie nodded, her gaze still fixed on the fire.

"Yeah. I think I've had enough excitement for one night." As they turned to leave, Maggie couldn't shake the feeling that someone was watching her. And as the shadows of the night deepened, she knew that the real danger was still out there, waiting.

Chapter Twenty-One: The Confrontation

The night had settled over Whitaker Farm like a thick blanket of darkness, with only the occasional gust of wind stirring the skeletal branches of the nearby trees. The farmhouse was quiet, save for the crackling of the fire that danced in the hearth.

Maggie stood near the window, gazing out into the inky blackness, her heart heavy with an unshakable sense of foreboding. Bear lay at her feet, his head resting on his paws, but even he seemed restless, his ears twitching at the slightest sound. The wind howled outside, causing the shutters to rattle against the windows. Maggie shivered, though the warmth from the fire should have been enough to keep her comfortable. There was something in the air tonight—something that set her nerves on edge. She couldn't quite put her finger on it, but it was there, lurking just beneath the surface, waiting. Then, out of the corner of her eye, she saw it—a flicker of movement near the barn. Her heart skipped a beat, her breath catching in her throat as she strained to see through the darkness. And then she saw him. Edward. He was standing just beyond the reach of the lantern light, his figure barely discernible in the shadows. But it was him. She could feel it.

"Daniel!" Maggie's voice was barely more than a whisper, but it was laced with urgency and fear.

She stepped back from the window, her hand instinctively reaching down to rest on Bear's head. The dog's ears perked up, and he lifted his head, a low growl rumbling in his chest. Daniel, seated by the fire, was on his feet in an instant. He crossed the room in a few quick strides, his face hardening as he followed Maggie's gaze out the window. His eyes locked onto the dark figure outside, and a muscle in his jaw twitched as anger flared inside him.

"I'll deal with him," Daniel said, his voice low and dangerous. He grabbed his coat and strode toward the door, his movements sharp and purposeful. "Stay inside."

Maggie watched as Daniel threw open the door and stepped out into the cold night. Bear was right on his heels, barking furiously as he bounded down the steps and onto the yard. Maggie felt a knot of anxiety tighten in her chest, but she stayed rooted in place, her eyes glued to the scene unfolding outside. The wind whipped through the yard, carrying the scent of wet earth and woodsmoke. Willow, the mare, stamped her hooves nervously in the paddock, her breath visible in the cold night air. She neighed softly, tossing her head as if sensing the tension that hung in the air. Daniel marched across the yard toward Edward, his fists clenched at his sides, his body taut with fury. Edward, standing with his hands in his coat pockets, didn't move as Daniel approached. The faint glow of the lanterns illuminated his face just enough for Maggie to see the cruel smirk that twisted his lips.

"What are you doing here, Edward?" Daniel growled, his voice low and threatening. "Haven't you caused enough damage?"

Edward's smile widened, and he took a step forward, his eyes gleaming with malice.

"I just came to see Maggie," he said smoothly, his voice dripping with condescension. "Surely there's no harm in that."

Daniel's patience snapped. Without warning, he lunged at Edward, his fist connecting with Edward's jaw in a sickening thud. Edward staggered back, caught off guard, but he quickly recovered, throwing a punch of his own. The two men crashed together, their bodies colliding with a force that echoed across the yard. Bear barked wildly, circling the fight, his sharp teeth bared as he growled at Edward. The sound of fists meeting flesh filled the air, along with grunts of pain and anger. Willow, still restless, reared up slightly in her paddock, her hooves kicking at the air as the tension in the yard mounted. Maggie stood frozen in the doorway, her heart pounding in her chest. She wanted to run out and stop them, but fear kept her rooted in place.

Then, out of the corner of her eye, she saw Hank, Sam, and Pete rushing from the barn, their faces pale with worry as they sprinted toward the fight.

"Stop them!" Hank shouted, his voice barely audible over the wind and the commotion.

He and Pete grabbed hold of Daniel, trying to pull him off Edward, while Sam moved to restrain Edward. But before anyone could intervene further, the deafening sound of a gunshot ripped through the night. The world seemed to slow down in that moment. Maggie's breath caught in her throat as she watched in horror. Time seemed to freeze as Sam fell to the ground, clutching his side, blood seeping through his fingers.

"No!" Maggie screamed, her hands flying to her mouth as she watched the scene unfold.

Bear barked wildly, rushing back to her side, his tail between his legs, whimpering with fear. Maggie felt a wave of helplessness wash over her as she saw the blood pooling beneath Sam's body. Daniel and Edward both stopped in their tracks, their faces pale as they registered what had happened.

Hank and Pete dropped to their knees beside Sam, trying to stop the bleeding, but the look of fear in their eyes told Maggie everything she needed to know—Sam was in grave danger.

Chapter Twenty-Two: The Doctor Arrives

The gunshot still echoed in Hank's ears as he galloped through the misty streets of Briarwood on Willow, his heart pounding. The cold night air stung his face, but he didn't care. All that mattered was reaching Dr. Jonas Miller before it was too late. Sensing the urgency, Willow flew down the road with a strength and speed that belied her size, her breath coming in quick, visible puffs in the chill. The rhythmic pounding of her hooves seemed to match the thudding of Hank's heart as the distance between the farm and the town grew shorter.

In the pale moonlight, the town of Briarwood looked eerie and still. The streets were deserted, and the mist hung low, swirling like ghostly tendrils as Hank guided Willow toward the edge of town, where Dr. Miller lived. It felt as though the night itself was holding its breath, waiting for what was to come.

By the time Hank reached the doctor's small, modest home, Willow's sides were heaving from the hard ride, but she stamped the ground impatiently as Hank dismounted, her eyes reflecting the lamplight with an almost knowing gleam. Hank rushed to the door, his heart in his throat, and pounded his fist against the wood.

"Dr. Miller! Open up, it's Hank!" he shouted, his voice hoarse with panic. There was a brief moment of silence before the door swung open, revealing the tall, lean figure of Dr. Jonas Miller. The doctor's sharp blue eyes, always so alert and calculating, immediately locked onto Hank, and his face, lined with age and experience, hardened at the sight of Hank's panic.

"Hank, what is it?" Dr. Miller asked, his voice gravelly but steady, though he was already moving to grab his medical bag from a nearby table. "It's Sam—he's been shot!"

Hank's words came out in a rush, his chest rising and falling rapidly as he tried to catch his breath. "We need you back at the farm right now. He's bleeding bad, Doc."

Dr. Miller's expression grew grim as he swung his heavy wool coat over his shoulders and grabbed his bag.

"How bad is it?" he asked, his voice low and urgent, but calm. This wasn't his first emergency, and his composed demeanor immediately reassured Hank. "He's losing a lot of blood," Hank said, his voice shaking. "Maggie's trying to stop it, but we don't know how long he has."

Without wasting another second, Dr. Miller strode out the door and mounted Willow behind Hank, the mare shifting under their combined weight but settling quickly as she turned back toward Whitaker Farm. As if sensing the desperation in the air, Willow galloped forward without hesitation, her hooves pounding against the dirt road as they raced back through the fog-shrouded streets. The ride back to the farm seemed longer than ever, despite Willow's swift pace. Hank clenched the reins tightly, his mind racing with thoughts of Sam, lying there on the cold ground, bleeding out. He couldn't lose his friend—not like this. He refused to let Sam's life slip away without a fight.

Back at Whitaker Farm, the farmhouse was a tense, chaotic scene. Inside, the air was thick with the smell of sweat, blood, and fear. Sam lay sprawled on the kitchen table, his face ashen, his breathing shallow. His shirt was soaked with blood, the red stark against the pale fabric. Maggie knelt beside him, her hands trembling as she pressed a rag to his side in a desperate attempt to stem the bleeding. Bear, ever loyal, paced nervously beside her, his whimpers growing louder with every passing second. He pressed his head against Maggie's leg, as though trying to comfort her, but Maggie barely noticed. Her eyes were fixed on Sam, her heart heavy with fear. Every second felt like an eternity as she waited for Hank to return with the doctor.

"Maggie," Sam groaned, his voice barely audible above the crackling fire in the hearth. His eyes fluttered open, and he winced in pain. "Is… is it bad?"

Tears stung Maggie's eyes as she looked down at him. "It's not that bad, Sam," she lied, her voice shaking as she tried to keep her emotions in check. "You're going to be just fine. Dr. Miller is on his way."

Sam's face twisted in pain, and his breathing grew more labored with each passing moment. Maggie felt a surge of helplessness wash over her as she tried to stop the blood that continued to seep through the cloth.

"Just hold on," she whispered, her hands trembling. "Hold on."

Pete stood near the door, his arms crossed over his chest as he stared at the floor, his face pale. Daniel, still reeling from the fight with Edward, paced back and forth near the window, his mind clouded with guilt. He should have stopped Edward sooner. He should have protected Sam. The weight of that guilt pressed down on him like a heavy stone, and he clenched his fists in frustration. Suddenly, the sound of hooves pounding against the ground broke through the tense silence, and Pete rushed to the door just as Hank and Dr. Miller arrived. Willow came to a halt, her sides heaving, and Hank jumped down, practically dragging the doctor toward the house.

"Maggie, I'm here!" Hank called as he pushed the door open, allowing Dr. Miller to rush inside.

Dr. Miller, tall and imposing, moved quickly to the table where Sam lay. His sharp blue eyes scanned the situation, taking in the sight of the blood-soaked cloths and the pallor of Sam's skin. He nodded once, his face grim but calm.

"Let me take over," he said, his voice steady. "We need to get him stable."

Maggie stepped back, her heart pounding as Dr. Miller set to work. Bear, sensing the shift in energy, whined softly and sat down beside Maggie, resting his head on her lap. She absentmindedly stroked his fur, drawing some small comfort from the loyal dog's presence. The doctor worked with swift, practiced hands, removing the blood-soaked bandages and cleaning the wound with antiseptic.

"The bullet went through," Dr. Miller said after a moment, his voice low and focused. "That's good. It didn't hit anything vital, but he's lost a lot of blood. We'll need to stop the bleeding and stitch him up. It's going to be a long night."

Maggie stood by, wringing her hands together, her eyes never leaving Sam's face. His breathing was shallow, his eyes half-closed as he fought to stay conscious. Bear, still by her side, nudged her gently with his nose, sensing her distress. She knelt down beside the dog, burying her face in his fur for a brief moment, grateful for his steady presence.

As Dr. Miller worked, the room was filled with an unbearable tension. Pete stood near the fire, his arms crossed tightly over his chest, while Hank hovered nearby, his face etched with worry. Daniel, still pacing near the window, finally stopped and leaned against the wall, his face pale with guilt and anger.

"This never should have happened," Daniel muttered under his breath, his fists clenching at his sides. "I should've stopped Edward sooner."

Maggie looked up at him, her eyes filled with sympathy and pain. "It's not your fault, Daniel," she said softly, her voice barely above a whisper. "None of this is your fault."

Daniel's jaw tightened, and he looked away, his heart heavy with guilt. But before he could respond, Dr. Miller finally stepped back, wiping his hands on a cloth as he surveyed his work.

"He's stable now," the doctor said, his voice still calm but with a note of relief. "He's going to need plenty of rest, but he'll pull through."

A collective sigh of relief filled the room. Maggie felt the weight lift from her chest as she sank into a nearby chair, exhaustion washing over her. Bear nuzzled her hand, and she smiled faintly, her heart swelling with gratitude for the loyal dog who had stayed by her side throughout the ordeal.

"Thank you, Dr. Miller," Maggie whispered, her voice thick with emotion. "I don't know what we would've done without you."

Dr. Miller gave her a small, reassuring nod. "Sam's a fighter," he said, his tone gentle but firm. "He'll pull through. Just keep him warm, and make sure he stays hydrated. I'll come by tomorrow to check on him."

As the tension in the room began to ease, Dr. Miller packed up his bag and prepared to leave. But before he stepped out the door, he paused, looking back at Maggie, Daniel, and the others with a serious expression.

"I'll be keeping an eye on Edward," Dr. Miller said, his voice low. "He's dangerous, and we can't let our guard down. You all be careful."

With that, the doctor turned and left, leaving the farmhouse in a heavy silence. Maggie sat quietly, her hand resting on Bear's head as she watched the fire crackle.

Chapter Twenty-Three: A New Chapter

The morning sunlight filtered gently through the thin curtains of the Whitaker Farm farmhouse, casting soft golden rays across the kitchen table where Sam lay resting. The tension of the previous night had finally eased, and the quiet stillness in the air was a welcome relief after hours of fear and uncertainty. Maggie entered the room, her steps quiet as she approached Sam's bedside. Pete, who had stayed up through the night, sat in a nearby chair, his head nodding slightly in exhaustion. The dark circles under his eyes told Maggie just how long and hard the night had been for all of them.

"How is he?" Maggie asked softly, not wanting to disturb Sam's rest. Pete blinked a few times, shaking off the weariness.

"He's stable," Pete replied, his voice thick with fatigue. "Made it through the night. Dr. Miller was right—he's strong."

Maggie felt a wave of relief wash over her, her shoulders sagging as she let out the breath she hadn't realized she was holding. She knelt beside the bed, gently touching Sam's arm. His face was still pale, but his breathing was steady, and for the first time since the shooting, there was color returning to his cheeks.

"He'll need time to heal," Maggie murmured, her voice filled with quiet gratitude. "But he'll pull through."

Outside, the day had begun to unfold in the usual way, with the soft sounds of Willow snorting in the paddock and the gentle rustling of the leaves in the trees. It was as if nature had sighed with relief after the long night. But Edward's shadow still hung over the farm, a reminder that their peace was fragile.

Later that morning, Sheriff Turner arrived at Whitaker Farm, his stern face marked with the weariness of the long hours spent tracking down Edward. His broad-brimmed hat cast a shadow over his weathered features, but his eyes were sharp with purpose.

"He's in custody now," the sheriff announced as he stepped inside.

Daniel and Maggie exchanged a glance, both feeling a small sense of justice being restored.

"Edward won't be causing any more trouble for a long while. The charges against him are serious enough that I don't expect him to see the light of day anytime soon."

Maggie let out a breath she didn't realize she had been holding. Finally, the threat that had loomed over her was gone, at least for now. But even as the sheriff's words offered reassurance, a flicker of doubt lingered in her chest—Edward had always been a dangerous man, and part of her feared what he might try next, even behind bars.

"Thank you, Sheriff," Daniel said, his voice steady but firm. "We'll sleep easier knowing he's locked up."

The sheriff nodded, his eyes flicking toward Sam, who was still resting in the other room.

"You all did well to get Dr. Miller here in time. Sam's lucky to have such a strong community around him."

With a final nod, the sheriff tipped his hat and left the farmhouse, the sound of his boots fading as he returned to town. The relief that came with Edward's arrest hung in the air like the first sign of dawn breaking after a long, stormy night.

By midday, the small town of Briarwood had settled into its familiar rhythm, and Hartwell Mercantile was bustling with customers preparing for the cooler days ahead. Maggie, though still shaken by the events of the previous days, found solace in the routine of running the store. The clink of the cash register, the smell of fresh produce, and the hum of customer conversations brought a sense of normalcy that she desperately needed. Ever the optimist, Clara joined Maggie behind the counter, her cheerful demeanor a welcome balm to Maggie's lingering worries. As Clara stacked fresh jars of preserves on the shelf, she glanced at Maggie, her eyes twinkling with curiosity.

"So," Clara began, her voice light and playful, "now that Edward's out of the picture, I assume things between you and Daniel are moving along nicely?"

Maggie smiled, a blush creeping into her cheeks. "We've been through a lot," she admitted, her fingers absentmindedly brushing a strand of hair behind her ear. "But yes, I think we've grown even closer."

Clara set the last jar down and turned to face Maggie, her expression softening.

"I'm happy for you, Maggie. You deserve happiness after everything that's happened." Maggie paused for a moment, her heart warming at Clara's words. She had been so caught up in the whirlwind of the past few weeks that she hadn't stopped to appreciate the love that had blossomed between her and Daniel. He had been her rock, standing by her side through every storm. Just as Clara was about to continue, the bell above the door jingled, and Maggie turned to see Daniel standing in the doorway, his presence filling the room with a quiet strength. He smiled as his eyes met Maggie's; for a moment, everything else faded away.

That evening, after the store had closed and the last rays of sunlight cast a warm glow over the town, Daniel led Maggie to a quiet spot by the riverbank just beyond the farm. The water shimmered under the soft light of the setting sun, and the gentle breeze rustled the tall grass around them. They had walked in comfortable silence, their hands intertwined as they made their way to the spot where Daniel often came to think. The peaceful sound of the flowing river was soothing, and Maggie felt a sense of calm wash over her as they stood by the water's edge.

"Maggie," Daniel said softly, turning to face her. His dark eyes were filled with warmth, but there was also a seriousness in his expression that caught Maggie's attention.

"Yes?" Maggie replied, her heart skipping a beat as she looked up at him. Daniel took a deep breath, his hand still holding hers as he reached into his coat pocket and pulled out a small, velvet box. The sight of it took Maggie's breath away, and her heart began to race.

"I've thought about this moment for a long time," Daniel began, his voice steady but filled with emotion. "You've been through so much, Maggie; through it all, you've shown strength, grace, and love. I can't imagine my life without you by my side."

Tears welled up in Maggie's eyes as she listened to his words, her heart swelling with love for the man standing before her. Daniel opened the box to reveal a delicate, beautiful ring—a simple gold band with a small, sparkling diamond at its center. The ring caught the fading light of the sun, its soft glow reflecting the love in Daniel's eyes.

"Maggie," Daniel continued, his voice filled with sincerity, "will you marry me?"

For a moment, the world seemed to stand still. The only sound was the gentle flow of the river and the soft whisper of the breeze through the trees. Maggie's heart was so full that she could barely find her voice.

"Yes," she whispered, her voice trembling with emotion. "Yes, Daniel, I will marry you."

A radiant smile spread across Daniel's face as he slipped the ring onto Maggie's finger. The fit was perfect, and as Maggie looked down at the ring, she felt a surge of happiness like she had never known before. Daniel pulled her into his arms, holding her close as the sun dipped below the horizon, casting the sky in shades of pink and gold.

Everything else faded away: Edward, the fear, the uncertainty. All that mattered was their love and the promise of a future together.

Chapter Twenty-Four: Shadows and Celebrations

The morning light bathed Whitaker Farm in a golden glow, the sun's warmth promising a fresh start after the tensions of the previous days. Inside, the mood was cautiously optimistic. Sam had made it through the night, and though weak, his recovery had begun. Pete was tending to him, ensuring his friend was as comfortable as possible. Downstairs, Maggie was greeted by the familiar, comforting sight of Bear curled up near the hearth. The shepherd mix thumped his tail lazily as Maggie moved around the kitchen, but his eyes remained sharp and alert.

Daniel had already gone out to tend to the animals, and the rhythmic clink of metal against metal could be heard from the barn, where Willow snorted softly as she waited for her morning feed. But even with the comfort of routine, Edward's shadow still loomed over the farm. Sheriff Turner had been clear—Edward was in custody, but his connections and volatile nature left a lingering sense of unease.

Later that morning, Sheriff Turner arrived at the farm, his face a mixture of relief and weariness. Maggie and Daniel met him outside, the cool autumn breeze rustling the leaves as they stood near the barn.

"Edward's been officially charged," the sheriff said, his voice gruff but firm. "Assault, attempted murder, and a list of other offenses. He's not getting out anytime soon."

Daniel, standing tall beside Maggie, nodded in approval. "That's good to hear," he said, though his voice was still tight.

He hadn't yet let go of the weight of what had happened, but at least now they could breathe a little easier. "Still," the sheriff added, glancing toward the town.

"Keep your wits about you. Edward has connections—people who might not be keen to let him stay behind bars. We're closely monitoring things, but I thought you should know." Maggie's heart sank slightly. Even with Edward locked up, the danger hadn't completely passed. She nodded her thanks to the sheriff, who tipped his hat and turned to leave, the sound of his boots crunching on the gravel the only sound in the otherwise quiet morning. As the sheriff rode away, Daniel turned to Maggie, his brow furrowed in thought.

"We'll keep watch," he said, his voice steady but laced with concern. "But for now, we can focus on what's ahead."

Maggie gave a small smile, appreciating Daniel's quiet strength. He had always been the one to look forward to pushing through challenges with determination. And now, more than ever, she was grateful for his unwavering presence.

By midday, Maggie found herself back at Hartwell Mercantile, where the comforting routine of running the store helped settle her nerves. The shop bustled with townsfolk preparing for the cooler months ahead, buying everything from jars of preserves to thick woolen blankets. The bell above the door chimed constantly, a reminder of the steady rhythm of life in Briarwood.

Clara, always the bright spark of the town, joined Maggie behind the counter, her hands busy restocking jars on the shelves. Her usual smile was broader today, her eyes twinkling with excitement as she worked.

"You look like you've got something on your mind," Maggie said, raising an eyebrow as she caught Clara's expression.

Clara set down a jar of blackberry preserves and turned to face Maggie, her grin widening. "Well, I hear there's been some excitement around here," she said teasingly. "You and Daniel—officially engaged, from what I've heard?"

Maggie blushed, her heart fluttering at the memory of Daniel's proposal by the riverbank. "Yes," she admitted, a soft smile playing on her lips. "It's true. He asked me last night."

Clara clapped her hands together, her joy evident. "I knew it! Oh, Maggie, that's wonderful news. The whole town will be thrilled to hear it."

Maggie laughed softly, a little overwhelmed by the thought of the town buzzing with the news of her engagement. "I didn't expect it to happen so soon," she said, her eyes drifting to the simple yet beautiful ring Daniel had given her. "But it feels... right. Like everything is falling into place."

Clara's smile softened as she leaned against the counter. "You deserve this, Maggie. After everything you've been through, it's about time you had some happiness."

Maggie felt a warmth spread through her chest at Clara's words. For so long, her life had been a series of trials and tribulations, but now, with Daniel by her side and the promise of a future together, she finally felt like she was on the cusp of something wonderful. The two women spent the rest of the afternoon discussing wedding plans—though Maggie insisted it was still too early to think about the details, Clara was more than happy to toss out ideas for dresses, venues, and even flowers. The lighthearted conversation was exactly what Maggie needed to distract her from the lingering thoughts of Edward and the dangers he posed.

As the day drew close and the shop began to quiet, Maggie thought back to the evening before, when Daniel had led her to the peaceful spot by the riverbank.

The memory of his proposal still filled her heart with warmth, the way the sun had set behind them, casting the world in soft hues of pink and gold. His words had been simple but heartfelt, and when he'd slipped the ring onto her finger, Maggie had felt an overwhelming sense of peace—a feeling that, no matter what happened, they would face it together. Daniel had always been a man of action, someone who cared deeply for the people around him, but last night, in that quiet moment, Maggie had seen a new side of him. A side that was vulnerable, hopeful, and completely in love. As the sun began to set outside the shop, casting long shadows across the floor, Maggie felt a sense of calm settle over her. No matter what Edward or his connections might try, she knew that she and Daniel could face it together. They had each other, and that was more than enough.

That evening, as Maggie returned to Whitaker Farm, she was greeted by the familiar sight of Bear waiting at the gate, his tail wagging as she approached. Willow stood in the paddock, her coat gleaming in the last rays of the setting sun. The farm, with all its familiar sights and sounds, had become a place of safety for Maggie—a place where she could imagine building her future with Daniel. Inside, Daniel was already preparing dinner, his strong hands working methodically as he chopped vegetables and stirred the pot on the stove. Maggie smiled as she watched him, feeling a warmth spread through her chest at the simple, comforting scene.

"Everything all right at the store?" Daniel asked, glancing over his shoulder as Maggie entered the kitchen.

"Busy as usual," she replied, leaning against the counter. "Clara was full of excitement about the engagement. I think she's already planning half the wedding."

Daniel chuckled, his dark eyes twinkling with amusement. "That sounds like Clara. Always ready to jump in with ideas."

Maggie crossed the room and slipped her arms around Daniel's waist, resting her head against his back. "I'm just glad we have something to look forward to," she said softly. "After everything that's happened... it feels good to have some joy."

Daniel turned around, wrapping his arms around her and pulling her close. "We've been through a lot, Maggie," he murmured, his voice low and tender. "But we're stronger for it. And now, we have the rest of our lives to look forward to."

Maggie looked up at him, her heart swelling with love. "I can't wait," she whispered, her lips brushing against his. As the evening wore on and the stars twinkled in the sky, Maggie felt a deep sense of peace settle over her. No matter what challenges lay ahead, she knew that she could face anything with Daniel by her side.

Chapter Twenty-Five: Gathering Storms

The air was crisp with the bite of early winter, carrying the scent of damp earth and fallen leaves that littered the paths around Whitaker Farm. The farm had always been a place of solace for Maggie, a refuge from the storms that had raged in her life, but today, even as the morning light bathed the fields in gold, she couldn't shake the feeling that something dark still lingered on the horizon. Willow, the faithful mare, stood quietly in her paddock, her coat glistening in the sunlight. Bear was by Maggie's side, his sharp eyes scanning the open fields as if he, too, sensed the unease that hung in the air. Maggie's fingers idly stroked his thick fur as she stood on the porch, her thoughts far from the farm.

Inside the house, the clatter of dishes and the low murmur of voices filled the space as Daniel finished breakfast with Pete and Sam. Sam was still recovering, though his color had returned, and he now moved with more confidence, even if he still needed assistance. Maggie's thoughts drifted back to the sheriff's visit. Edward may have been in custody, but there was no guarantee that his influence had been entirely cut off. The sheriff's warning about strangers asking questions gnawed at her the most. There was always a possibility that Edward had allies, people who would be willing to continue his vendetta, even from the shadows. The idea of unknown threats moving quietly in the background sent a chill down her spine.

The door creaked open behind her, and Daniel stepped out, his face calm but his eyes carrying the same quiet concern she felt. He wrapped his arms around her from behind, pulling her close as they stood together on the porch, looking out over the fields.

"Anything on your mind?" Daniel asked softly, his chin resting on her shoulder.

Maggie sighed, leaning back into his warmth. "Just… everything, I suppose. It feels like we're waiting for something to happen, and I hate not knowing what it is."

Daniel kissed her, his arms tightening around her. "We've been through worse, Maggie. We'll get through this, too. Edward's behind bars, and whatever's coming next, we'll be ready."

Maggie nodded, appreciating Daniel's steady resolve, but the knot in her stomach remained. She glanced down at Bear, who was alertly watching the horizon. His ears perked as if he sensed something far off in the distance.

"We should get into town soon," Daniel said after a moment, his voice breaking the silence. "I need to check on the supplies for the winter, and we could both use the distraction."

Maggie smiled weakly, grateful for his suggestion. "You're right. A trip to town might help clear my head."

The ride into Briarwood was peaceful, but an unmistakable chill was in the air. The trees lining the road were mostly bare, their branches twisting upward like skeletal fingers. Willow's hooves echoed against the hard-packed dirt as she trotted along, her breath visible in the cold. When they reached town, Briarwood was alive with the usual hum of activity.

Hartwell Mercantile bustled with people preparing for the coming winter, stocking up on firewood, heavy blankets, and jars of preserves. The store was a hub of life in Briarwood, and today was no different. As Maggie dismounted and tied Willow to the post outside the store, she glanced around, scanning the familiar faces of the townsfolk. It felt comforting to see people going about their daily routines, but there was also a hint of unease, as though the town was holding its breath, waiting for something to disrupt the fragile peace.

Daniel helped her down from the saddle, his hand lingering on hers for a moment before they walked into the store together. The warmth inside was a welcome contrast to the chilly air outside, and the smell of fresh bread and warm spices filled the air, bringing a sense of comfort that momentarily eased Maggie's worries. As they entered, Clara waved from behind the counter, her face lighting up with a bright smile.

"Maggie! Daniel! It's good to see you both." Maggie returned the smile, grateful for Clara's ever-present cheer. "It's good to see you too, Clara," she replied as she approached the counter. The store was busy, but Clara always seemed to find time to chat, and today was no exception. She handed a customer a sack of flour before turning her full attention to Maggie.

"How are things on the farm?" Clara asked, her eyes sparkling with curiosity. Maggie hesitated for a moment, glancing at Daniel, who was busy talking to another man about supplies for the winter. She lowered her voice and leaned in slightly toward Clara.

"Things are fine… mostly. But Sheriff Turner recently mentioned some strangers asking questions about Edward."

Clara's brow furrowed, her cheerful expression slipping for a moment. "Strangers? What kind of questions?"

Maggie shook her head, biting her lip. "The sheriff didn't say much, just that we should be careful. It's… unnerving, to say the least."

Clara's face softened with understanding, and she reached across the counter to give Maggie's hand a reassuring squeeze.

"Edward's behind bars, Maggie. He can't hurt you anymore. And as for these strangers, we've got a good sheriff and a strong community. We'll be all right."

Maggie nodded, though the weight of her worries still lingered.

"I know. It's just hard not to think about what might happen next."

Clara gave her a knowing smile. "You've got too much to look forward to, Maggie. Don't let fear steal your joy."

As the afternoon wore on, Daniel and Maggie finished their errands and prepared to head back to the farm. But just as they were about to leave, Sheriff Turner approached them, his face lined with concern.

"I've heard more talk," the sheriff said, his voice low as they stepped away from the crowd. "A couple of men have been spotted asking about Edward again—seems they're not from around here. It could be nothing, but I'm watching it."

Maggie's heart sank at the news, and she exchanged a worried glance with Daniel.

"Do you think they're connected to him?" she asked, her voice barely above a whisper.

Sheriff Turner nodded slowly. "It's possible. Edward had friends in high places before all of this. We're watching for any signs of trouble, but I wanted to make sure you're prepared. Stay alert."

Maggie nodded, the sheriff's words deepening the knot of anxiety that had been building inside her. "Thank you for letting us know, Sheriff."

As the sheriff tipped his hat and turned to leave, Daniel placed a reassuring hand on Maggie's shoulder.

"We'll be careful," he said quietly, though his jaw was determined. "Let's head home."

The ride back to Whitaker Farm was quieter than usual, the weight of the sheriff's warnings pressing heavily on Maggie's mind. As they reached the farm, the last light of day faded, casting long shadows across the fields. Bear greeted them at the gate, his tail wagging as he sniffed at the wind, alert to every sound.

That evening, after a quiet dinner, Maggie and Daniel sat together on the porch, their hands intertwined as they watched the stars blink into the darkening sky. The chill in the air had deepened, but the warmth of Daniel's presence and the comfort of Bear lying at their feet brought Maggie a sense of peace, even as her mind raced with thoughts of what might be coming.

"I know it's hard not to worry," Daniel said softly, his voice steady in the quiet night.

"But we'll get through this, Maggie. Whatever Edward's trying to do, we'll face it together."

Maggie leaned into him, grateful for his strength. "I know," she whispered, her heart swelling with love. "As long as we have each other, we can face anything."

The world felt still for a moment, as though time had paused just for them. The stars above twinkled softly, and the cool breeze whispered through the trees, carrying the distant promise of winter with it. But even in the peaceful quiet of the night, Maggie couldn't shake the feeling that the gathering storm was drawing ever closer.

Chapter Twenty-Six: The Winds of Despair

The winds howled through Whitaker Farm, rattling the windows and tearing through the trees with a fierce, untamed power. The evening had started peacefully enough, with Maggie and Daniel finishing up dinner, but as the night deepened, the wind had picked up, transforming the once-quiet night into a stormy, unsettling scene. Maggie stood by the window, her brow furrowed as she watched the trees bend under the force of the gusts. Bear, usually so calm, was pacing near the door, his ears perked and his body tense. There was something about the night that felt different—ominous, even.

"Daniel," Maggie called out, her voice barely audible above the wind's roar. "I think we should check the barn. This weather might spook the animals."

Daniel, who had been busy stacking wood by the fire, looked up, his face mirroring her concern.

"You're right. I'll go check on Willow and the others. You stay inside—no sense in both of us braving this wind."

Maggie nodded, but a sense of unease twisted in her chest.

"Be careful." As Daniel slipped on his coat and stepped outside, Bear followed him to the door, barking at the howling wind. Maggie watched as Daniel disappeared into the swirling darkness, the lantern's light barely illuminating his path. She turned back to the kitchen, trying to shake the feeling that something wasn't right.

A few minutes passed in tense silence, with the wind growing louder, rattling the shutters as if trying to break through. Maggie stood at the counter, her hands trembling as she prepared tea, trying to focus on the simple task to calm her nerves. Bear, still uneasy, began to whine softly, his gaze fixed on the door. Suddenly, a loud crash sounded from outside—metal against metal, the sound of something falling hard. Maggie's heart leaped into her throat, and before she could think, she rushed toward the door, throwing it open to peer out into the darkness.

"Daniel?" she called out, her voice lost in the wind.

There was no answer. The wind whipped her hair around her face as she stepped onto the porch, squinting into the night, trying to make out any shapes in the swirling storm. But all she saw was darkness, the shadows moving unnaturally under the force of the wind. Without warning, a rough hand clamped over her mouth from behind, pulling her backward. Maggie's eyes widened in terror as she struggled, but her captor was too strong, dragging her off the porch and into the shadows before she could scream.

Bear barked wildly, his frantic howls swallowed by the wind as he lunged at Maggie's captor. But a sharp kick sent the dog yelping away, and within seconds, Maggie was thrown into the back of a wagon, the door slamming shut behind her.

Her heart pounded in her chest, and fear clawed at her throat as she realized she was being taken—kidnapped by the same unknown force that had threatened her for so long.

Meanwhile, in the small town jail where Edward had been held, an eerie quiet hung in the air, punctuated only by the distant howl of the wind outside. Sheriff Turner had been making his rounds, checking on the cells, when he noticed something strange in Edward's cell. The man who had caused so much pain, who had always been defiant and full of malice, was unnervingly silent.

"Sullivan," Sheriff Turner called to his deputy. "Something's off here."

The sheriff approached the bars of Edward's cell, his heart sinking as he saw the crude noose tied to the beam above. Edward hung limply from the makeshift rope, his body swaying slightly in the stillness of the cell.

"Sullivan!" the sheriff barked, his voice filled with alarm. "He's hanged himself!"

The deputy rushed over, but it was too late. Edward was dead, his final act of cowardice robbing them of any chance for justice. Sheriff Turner stood there, his jaw clenched in frustration and disbelief. This was not how things were supposed to end—not with Edward escaping his fate by his own hand. But as the sheriff stared at Edward's lifeless body, a sickening realization hit him.

Back at Whitaker Farm, Daniel was finishing his check on the animals when Bear's frantic barking reached his ears. He rushed back to the house, his heart racing as he saw Bear circling the porch, barking wildly into the darkness. Something was wrong. His gut told him so.

"Maggie!" Daniel shouted as he burst through the door, but the house was eerily silent.

His eyes scanned the room, searching for her, but there was no sign of Maggie. The lantern on the table flickered, casting long shadows across the walls, but the only sound was the relentless wind battering the house. Panic surged through him.

"Maggie!" he shouted again, louder this time, but the only response was Bear's desperate barking.

Without wasting another second, Daniel grabbed the lantern from the table and rushed outside, his heart pounding as he followed Bear's lead. The dog's nose was on the ground, his pace frantic as he sniffed the air, leading Daniel toward the back of the house. There, in the mud, Daniel found signs of a struggle—boot prints in the dirt, the faint marks of wagon wheels leading away from the house. His heart sank as the pieces began to fall into place.

"Maggie's been taken," Daniel whispered to himself, the realization hitting him like a punch to the gut. He fell to his knees in the dirt, his breath coming in ragged gasps as his mind raced.

"She's gone…"

For a moment, the world seemed to spin around him, the wind howling in his ears like a cruel reminder of the danger that had swept into their lives. But then, as the fear threatened to consume him, something stronger surged to the surface—determination. He would find her. He had to. Daniel stood up, his resolve hardening as he looked down at Bear, whose eyes were filled with a similar desperation.

"We're going to get her back," Daniel muttered, his voice filled with quiet fury. "No matter what it takes."

With the lantern in hand and Bear at his side, Daniel followed the wagon tracks into the storm, his heart pounding with fear and fury. Maggie was out there, somewhere in the darkness, and he wouldn't stop until he found her. Daniel's heart pounded with fear and determination as they pressed on into the swirling darkness. Somewhere out there, in the clutches of unknown hands, Maggie was fighting for her life, and he would not stop until he brought her back.

Chapter Twenty-Seven: The Race for Rescue

The wind whipped at their faces, making it hard to see, but Bear kept a steady pace beside them, his nose to the ground, following the faint wagon tracks quickly erased by the storm. Clara clung to her reins, her face pale but resolute. She had never been involved in such a dire situation, but her loyalty to Maggie was fierce.

"We're going to find her, Daniel," she called out over the wind, though her voice shook slightly. "We have to."

Daniel didn't respond. His jaw set as he urged his horse forward. Every minute that passed felt like an eternity. His mind raced with horrible images of what could be happening to Maggie, but he pushed them aside, focusing on the task at hand—finding her. Hank and Pete rode close behind, their lanterns casting flickering light on the path ahead. They were seasoned in the ways of the land, and despite the storm, they knew how to track through rough terrain. Still, the wind made it difficult to keep the trail, and more than once, they had to stop to reassess the tracks.

"Here!" Pete shouted, pointing to a fresh set of wheel marks that veered off the main road and into the dense woods to the east. "They've gone this way."

Daniel's pulse quickened. "We're getting closer," he muttered, urging his horse into a faster trot.

Bear barked as he ran ahead, his ears perked, his body low to the ground as he followed the scent.

Back in Briarwood, Sheriff Turner and Deputy Sullivan were still reeling from the shock of Edward's suicide. The eerie stillness of the jail cell, punctuated by the sound of the wind rattling the windowpanes, had left them both unsettled.

"This doesn't feel right," the sheriff muttered, rubbing a hand over his weathered face. "Edward hanging himself now, after everything... there's something we're not seeing."

As they worked to remove Edward's body from the cell, a young boy from the outskirts of town burst into the sheriff's office, out of breath and wide-eyed.

"Sheriff! Sheriff!" he cried. "They've taken Miss Maggie!"

Sheriff Turner's heart sank as he turned to the boy.

"What do you mean, son? Who's taken her?"

"I saw it from the hill—men in a wagon, and they grabbed her! Took her out toward the woods!" The boy's words tumbled out, his face pale with fear. The sheriff wasted no time.

"Sullivan, get the horses saddled. We're going after her."

Within minutes, the sheriff and his deputy were riding hard in the direction the boy had indicated, the storm making the journey difficult. They knew they were racing against time—if Edward had accomplices, they wouldn't stop at just kidnapping.

The further they ventured into the woods, the darker and more treacherous the path became. The dense trees swayed violently in the wind, their branches reaching out like twisted arms, making the narrow trail even more dangerous.

"Stay close!" Daniel shouted over the wind as he maneuvered his horse around a fallen branch. Bear ran ahead, and his ears flattened against his head as he followed the scent. Suddenly, Bear stopped his nose to the ground, sniffing furiously. He barked, and Daniel's heart leaped with hope.

"He's found something!" They dismounted quickly, their lanterns barely illuminating the small clearing where the wagon tracks ended. There were signs of a struggle—disturbed leaves, a piece of torn fabric caught on a branch—but no sign of Maggie.

"Spread out!" Daniel ordered, his voice thick with desperation. "She's close!"

Clara, her heart racing, followed Hank as they searched through the trees.

"Maggie!" she called out, her voice trembling. "Maggie, where are you?"

The wind roared in response, but there was no answer. Daniel knelt by the torn fabric, his fingers brushing over it. It was from Maggie's shawl—the one she had been wearing earlier that evening. His heart clenched. She had been here recently. As they spread out, hooves and raised voices came from behind.

Sheriff Turner and Sullivan rode into the clearing, their faces grim. "Saw the boy in town—he said Maggie's been taken," the sheriff said as he dismounted.

His sharp eyes scanned the area, taking in the signs of struggle.

"Looks like we're on the right trail." Daniel stood, his hands clenched into fists. "We have to find her, Sheriff. They could be anywhere."

"We'll find her," the sheriff said, calm but determined. "But we need to be smart about it. This storm's not helping, and we don't know what we're dealing with."

Just when hope seemed to be fading, Bear barked sharply, running toward the edge of the clearing. He stopped at a dense thicket, his nose to the ground, pawing at the dirt. Daniel rushed over, his heart pounding in his chest.

"What is it, boy?" As Daniel pushed through the undergrowth, his lantern cast a faint light on something that made his blood run cold—another set of wagon tracks, hidden in the thick brush, leading deeper into the forest.

"They're trying to throw us off the trail," Hank said grimly as he joined Daniel. "But they didn't count on Bear."

Without wasting another second, Daniel mounted his horse again.

"We keep going. We're close."

The group pressed on, following the new trail deeper into the woods. The storm raged around them, but their determination was stronger. Every passing second felt like a lifetime, but Daniel held on to one thought: finding Maggie. He refused to let anything happen to her. As they rode through the twisting paths, the sound of distant voices carried through the wind—low, rough voices, too far to make out clearly, but unmistakably human. Daniel's pulse quickened.

"There!" Pete pointed ahead, where a flicker of firelight broke through the trees. "They've got a camp up ahead!"

Daniel urged his horse forward, but Sheriff Turner held up a hand, signaling for caution. "We need to approach carefully. If they see us coming, they might hurt her."

With hearts pounding, they dismounted and moved quietly through the trees, Bear leading the way with his nose to the ground. The closer they got, the clearer the voices became.

"She's worth more alive than dead," one of the voices said, rough and menacing.

"I don't care about that," another voice growled. "We do what we came to do and get out of here."

Daniel's hands tightened around his lantern as the firelight revealed a small group of men huddled around a bound figure—Maggie, her wrists tied, her eyes wide with fear. The sight of her sent a surge of fury through Daniel.

"We're getting her out of there," he whispered to the sheriff. Sheriff Turner nodded, his jaw set.

"On my signal."

With a swift and silent motion, Sheriff Turner signaled the group to move in. Bear darted forward, barking ferociously, startling the men around the fire. The moment of confusion was all Daniel needed. He and Hank rushed forward, guns drawn, while Pete and Clara circled to cut off any escape. The sheriff and his deputy moved in quickly, weapons raised, shouting for the men to stand down. The kidnappers, caught off guard by the sudden assault, scrambled to grab their weapons, but it was too late. They were surrounded in a matter of seconds, with nowhere to run.

Daniel reached Maggie in an instant, pulling her into his arms and cutting the ropes that bound her wrists. Her face was pale, her body trembling, but relief flooded through both of them the moment their eyes met.

"Daniel…" Maggie's voice was barely a whisper, but it was filled with gratitude and disbelief.

"I've got you," Daniel whispered, holding her close. "You're safe now."

With the kidnappers subdued and the storm finally beginning to ease, Daniel, Maggie, and the others returned to Whitaker Farm. The danger had passed for now, but the shadow of what had happened lingered in the air. As they rode back under the clearing sky, Daniel held Maggie close, his heart full of relief and fury. Edward might be gone, but the darkness he had brought into their lives had not yet been fully extinguished. But for now, Maggie was safe. And that was all that mattered.

Chapter Twenty-Eight: Unveiling the Darkness

The dawn broke slowly over Whitaker Farm, casting a soft, muted light on the fields. Inside, the tension lingered like a thick fog, despite the calm after the storm. Maggie sat by the fire, her hands wrapped around a cup of tea, though the warmth barely reached her. Bear lay by her feet, his head resting on her lap, as if sensing her need for comfort.

Across the room, Daniel stood near the window, watching the early morning light with a hardened expression. The previous night's events had left them both shaken, but now the truth needed to come to light.

"They'll talk," Daniel said softly, though his voice had a sharp edge. "They'll tell us why they took you."

Maggie nodded, her fingers tightening around the cup.

"I still can't understand why. What did they want from me?" Before Daniel could respond, a knock at the door interrupted them. Sheriff Turner stepped inside, his face grim. "We've got the men in custody," he said, his voice low. "They're not talking much yet, but we'll get the truth out of them."

In the small Briarwood jailhouse, the three men who had taken Maggie sat in a dimly lit cell. Jed Slade, their leader, leaned against the wall, his scarred face a mask of indifference. His two accomplices, Amos Tate and Billy "Red" Thompson, sat beside him, each looking equally worn by the night's events. They knew the law had finally caught up with them.

Sheriff Turner stood just outside the bars, his arms crossed as he eyed the three men. Daniel stood beside him, barely able to contain his anger as he looked at the men who had nearly destroyed his life.

"We know Edward Townsend was behind this," the sheriff said, his voice cold. "But now he's dead. You'd better start explaining why you took Maggie."

Jed Slade, the scar-faced leader, snorted and glanced at Daniel. "It wasn't personal, farmer boy. We were just following orders. Edward had debts, which didn't disappear when he went to jail."

Daniel took a step forward, his fists clenched. "So you kidnapped her to settle a debt?"

Slade shrugged. "Edward owed some dangerous people a lot of money. He thought if he had leverage, he could buy himself some time. We were supposed to take the girl, hold her for ransom. You've got land. Figured you'd pay up quick if it meant getting her back in one piece."

The sheriff narrowed his eyes at Slade. "Who was Edward dealing with?"

Slade's sneer faded slightly. "He owed a lot of people. But this debt was to men you don't want to cross. They wanted their money and didn't care how they got it. They figured we'd handle things for him when Edward went to jail."

Amos Tate, the hulking man sitting beside Slade, had remained silent during most of the exchange. His massive frame barely fit on the narrow bench, and his downcast eyes hinted at a man who had been dragged into a world he didn't fully understand. He had been the muscle in the operation. His size alone meant to intimidate anyone who stood in their way.

"I didn't want to hurt the girl," Amos finally muttered, his voice low and gravelly. "I just needed the money. I've done time before, and I didn't want to go back. Slade said it was an easy job."

Daniel's fury rose. "Easy? You call kidnapping and terrorizing a woman easy?"

Amos shifted uncomfortably, unable to meet Daniel's gaze. "It wasn't supposed to go this far."

The third man, Billy "Red" Thompson, was younger than the other two, his wiry frame and red hair making him look out of place among the hardened criminals. His wide, frightened eyes darted between his captors and the sheriff. Billy had fallen in with the wrong crowd, desperate for a way out of his poverty-stricken life.

"I didn't want to do it," Billy stammered, his voice shaking. "I swear! I was just supposed to drive the wagon. I thought we'd grab her, get some money, and leave. I didn't know it would be like this."

Sheriff Turner turned his gaze on the young man. "You still took part in it. And you'll answer for it." Billy shrunk back, his hands trembling.

"I'm sorry," he whispered, but the words felt hollow.

With the men's confessions, the sheriff pieced together the events leading to Maggie's kidnapping. Edward Townsend, desperate to escape his mounting debts, had planned to ransom Maggie, hoping to buy time before his creditors closed in. But once he was arrested, Edward's paranoia grew. The men he owed were not the kind to wait for payment, and the weight of it all drove him to take his own life.

"Edward knew what was coming," Sheriff Turner said, his voice tight.

"He must've realized there was no way out. Hanging himself was his way of escaping the inevitable."

Daniel clenched his fists. "Coward."

The sheriff nodded. "Maybe. But Edward wasn't the only one with something to lose. His debts are still out there, and the people he owed are likely still looking for their money. We need to stay alert. This might not be over."

Later that day, Jonathan Townsend, Edward's older brother, arrived in Briarwood to claim the body. Jonathan was an imposing figure; his tall frame and sharp features made him stand out in the small town. He had come with a purpose, and it wasn't just to collect Edward's remains.

Sheriff Turner was met with barely restrained fury when he stepped out of his office to meet Jonathan. Jonathan's dark eyes were cold as they bore into the sheriff.

"You let my brother die," Jonathan said, his voice low and dangerous. "You were supposed to keep him safe."

The sheriff's jaw tightened. "Edward hanged himself. There was nothing anyone could've done to stop him."

Jonathan stepped closer, his voice growing more menacing. "You're going to regret this, Turner. My family won't forget how you let him down. And we'll make sure you pay for it."

The sheriff didn't flinch. "You're welcome to file a complaint with the town council. But if you're threatening me, Jonathan, you'd better think twice."

Jonathan's sneer deepened. "This isn't over. You'll see."

As Jonathan stalked off, Sheriff Turner let out a slow breath. The Townsend family had deep connections, and Jonathan's threats were not to be taken lightly. The storm surrounding Edward's death was far from over.

Back at Whitaker Farm, Daniel and Maggie sat together by the fire as the sun began to set. The revelations about Edward's debts and the men who had taken her left a bitter taste in both of their mouths. Maggie leaned her head against Daniel's shoulder, her body still trembling slightly from the fear that lingered.

"Do you think they'll come after us again?" she asked quietly, her voice filled with unease.

Daniel wrapped his arm around her, holding her close. "I don't know," he admitted, his heart heavy with the weight of the unknown.

"But if they do, we'll be ready." Maggie closed her eyes, trying to push away the lingering fear. "I just want this to be over."

"We'll get through this," Daniel murmured, kissing her forehead. "Whatever comes next, we'll face it together."

Chapter Twenty-Nine: Love in Blood

The farm quieted as the golden afternoon light faded into evening, but the warmth and excitement inside the farmhouse lingered. After dinner, Maggie and Daniel sat at the table, their fingers intertwined as they reviewed more wedding details. The thought of their future together brought a smile to both their faces, even after all the trials they had been through.

Clara and Pete, on the other hand, found themselves lingering by the barn. The day's work was done, but neither seemed ready to say goodnight. Pete was adjusting the harnesses, his hands moving expertly over the worn leather, while Clara stood nearby, watching him with an admiring smile.

"I've never seen anyone handle horses as well as you do," Clara said, breaking the comfortable silence between them.

Pete looked up at her, his grin widening. "Years of practice. Besides, I think Willow here likes the attention."

Clara laughed softly, stepping closer to stroke Willow's nose.

"Well, I think she knows when she's in good hands." Something was in the air between them, a quiet understanding that neither needed to speak aloud. They had spent more time together in recent weeks, their friendship deepening into something more, though neither had yet found the courage to name it. Pete put down the harness he was working on and turned to Clara, his expression more serious now.

"Clara, I've been meaning to say something."

Clara looked up, her heart skipping a beat. "What is it?"

Pete rubbed the back of his neck, suddenly looking a bit unsure of himself. "I've been thinking a lot about... us. You've been spending more time here at the farm, and... well, I'm glad you have. It feels right, you know? Like you belong here."

Clara's cheeks flushed, her pulse quickening at his words. She had felt it too—the sense of belonging, the growing bond between them—but hearing Pete say it aloud made her heart flutter in a way she hadn't expected.

"I've felt the same," Clara admitted, her voice soft.

"I didn't realize how much this place—how much you—mean to me." Pete's eyes softened, and for a moment, they stood in silence, the unspoken feelings between them clear as day. Then, without hesitation, Pete reached out and took Clara's hand in his. His grip was firm yet gentle, grounding her in the moment.

"I don't want to rush anything," Pete said, his voice low and sincere. "But I wanted you to know. You mean a lot to me, Clara. More than I've been able to say."

Clara's heart swelled with emotion. She had always been the kind of woman who prided herself on being independent, but in this moment, she realized that she had found something special with Pete—something she hadn't been looking for but now couldn't imagine being without.

"I'm not in any rush either," Clara replied, squeezing his hand. "But I'm glad we're on the same page."

Pete's smile grew, and in that quiet, shared moment, they both knew they had taken the first step toward something deeper. As they stood there, hand in hand, the barn around them quiet and warm, the future suddenly seemed a little brighter.

Inside the farmhouse, Maggie and Daniel were lost in their wedding plans, their conversation filled with laughter and excitement. Maggie had been making notes all evening, her ideas for the ceremony growing by the minute.

"I was thinking," Maggie began, tapping her pencil against the notebook, "what if we had the ceremony near the big oak tree by the pond? It's always been one of my favorite spots on the farm, and it's so peaceful there."

Daniel's eyes sparkled with affection as he listened. "That sounds perfect. We could string up lanterns, maybe even have a small arch with flowers."

Maggie nodded eagerly, her imagination already painting the picture. "Yes! And we could have a few benches for the guests. We'll keep it small, just close friends. I want it to feel intimate."

Daniel chuckled. "Knowing Clara, she'll probably insist on helping with all the decorations. She's been as excited about this wedding as we are."

Maggie grinned. "I'm counting on it. I wouldn't want to do this without her."

The two continued to plan, their voices filled with warmth as they talked about the ceremony, the flowers, and even the food they would serve. Maggie's heart swelled with love every time she looked at Daniel. After all the danger and uncertainty they had faced, the thought of finally being his wife filled her with a sense of peace she hadn't felt in years.

"I can't wait to marry you," Maggie said softly, reaching across the table to take Daniel's hand. Daniel's smile was tender as he squeezed her hand in return.

"Neither can I. It feels like we've been waiting forever."

The sound of the front door opening interrupted their conversation, and Clara and Pete stepped inside, both looking slightly flushed from the cool evening air and the emotions that had passed between them.

"You two are still at it?" Pete teased, walking over to the table. "I'd say you've got the wedding all planned by now."

"Almost," Maggie said with a grin. "There's still a lot to do, but it's coming together."

Clara sat down beside Maggie, her eyes shining with excitement. "What can I help with? I'm ready to start decorating whenever you need me!"

Maggie laughed. "I knew I could count on you! We're thinking about having the ceremony by the oak tree near the pond. You and Pete could help with setting up the benches and lanterns."

Pete nodded. "We're happy to help. Anything to make sure it's perfect for you two."

As they all sat together, talking and laughing about the upcoming wedding, there was a sense of joy and anticipation that filled the room. The challenges they had faced were not forgotten, but for now, they were surrounded by love and the promise of a brighter future.

Later that night, after the farmhouse had quieted down and everyone had gone to bed, Maggie sat by the window in her room, gazing out at the moonlit fields. Willow stood quietly in the paddock, and the soft sound of crickets filled the air.

Daniel entered the room, his steps quiet as he approached her. "What are you thinking about?" he asked, his voice gentle as he wrapped his arms around her from behind.

Maggie leaned back against him, closing her eyes for a moment.

"Just everything. How far we've come. How close we were to losing everything."

Daniel kissed the top of her head, his arms tightening around her.

"We made it through, Maggie. And now we're building something even stronger."

Maggie smiled, her heart filled with love. "I can't wait to start this new chapter with you."

As they stood together, bathed in the soft glow of the moonlight, the future stretched before them, filled with hope, love, and the knowledge that they would face them together no matter what challenges lay ahead.

Chapter Thirty: A Day of Surprises

The crisp autumn air swept through Whitaker Farm, carrying the scent of hay and apples from the orchard. The days had grown shorter, and the wedding was fast approaching, casting a sense of excitement and busyness over the farm. But today was different. It felt like one of those rare, perfect days where everything was going right. Maggie was outside brushing down Willow, the beautiful mare whinnying softly in appreciation. The sun was just high enough to cast a golden light over the fields, and Maggie smiled as she worked, happy to lose herself in the quiet rhythm of farm life. Beside her, Bear padded around the paddock, occasionally sniffing at the ground or trotting back to her side, his tail wagging contentedly.

Daniel was seated at the kitchen table inside the farmhouse with Pete, both men working on finalizing the repairs to the barn ahead of the wedding. Pete had grown increasingly at ease around the farm and especially around Clara, who was in the garden picking fresh vegetables for dinner with Clara herself.

"The barn's coming along," Pete said, wiping sweat from his brow. "Should be finished in time for the wedding."

Daniel nodded with satisfaction. "Good. Maggie's been talking about stringing up lanterns out there. We'll need to make sure the place is solid before we start setting everything up."

Pete's eyes flicked to the window, where the vegetable patch crouched Clara, her fingers lightly brushing the tops of the plants. A soft smile touched his lips, and Daniel noticed.

"She's special, isn't she?" Daniel asked with a knowing look.

Pete blushed, scratching the back of his neck. "Yeah, she is. I didn't expect to feel this way, but Clara... she's something else."

"You should tell her how you feel," Daniel said, his tone serious but encouraging. "You never know how much time you have."

Pete nodded, his eyes lingering on Clara for a moment longer. "I think I will."

Just as Pete and Daniel finished their conversation, the sound of hooves clattering on the dirt path announced Sheriff Turner's arrival. He rode into the yard, his horse kicking up dust as he slowed to a halt. Maggie looked up from brushing Willow and gave a small wave, but the sheriff's expression was unusually grim.

Daniel and Pete stepped outside to greet him, sensing something was amiss.

"Sheriff, everything all right?" Daniel asked, his brow furrowing.

Sheriff Turner dismounted, his boots hitting the ground with a heavy thud. "I've got some news," he said, his voice low. "Jonathan Townsend's been causing a stir in town. He's been talking to some folks—people who ain't exactly friendly. Looks like he's not letting go of what happened to his brother."

Daniel's face hardened. "Is he making threats?"

The sheriff nodded grimly. "Not outright, but he's got people whispering in his ear, stirring up trouble. I'm worried it's only a matter of time before he does something stupid."

Pete frowned, glancing toward the house where Clara and Maggie had joined them, sensing the tension in the air. "What do you think he'll do?" Pete asked, crossing his arms.

Sheriff Turner sighed. "I don't know yet, but I'd keep an eye out. If Jonathan's looking for revenge, I don't want anyone on this farm caught in the crossfire."

Maggie's heart sank at the thought. After everything they had been through, the idea of more trouble brewing was enough to send a chill down her spine.

"We'll be ready," Daniel said, his voice firm. "If Jonathan comes after us, we won't back down."

Despite the sheriff's warning, the rest of the afternoon passed peacefully. The group gathered outside to enjoy the cool evening air as the sun began to set, casting the fields in a warm golden light. Bear ran circles around the group, barking happily as he chased after Willow, who trotted lazily near the fence.

Clara and Pete stood to the side, watching the sun dip below the horizon. Pete glanced at Clara, his heart pounding as he tried to muster the courage to say what had been on his mind for days.

"You know," Pete began, his voice soft but steady, "I've been meaning to tell you something."

Clara looked up at him, her blue eyes curious. "What is it?"

Pete took a deep breath, his hands slightly trembling as he reached for hers. "I've never felt like I belonged anywhere... until I met you. Being here at the farm, getting to know you—it's changed everything for me. I want you to know that I care about you, Clara. More than I've cared about anyone in a long time."

Clara's heart fluttered at his words, her cheeks flushing slightly as she smiled up at him. "I care about you too, Pete. I didn't expect to find something like this, especially not here, but... I'm glad I did."

For a moment, they stood in the fading light, the air between them filled with unspoken promises and the warmth of new love. Pete squeezed her hand, and Clara leaned into him, her heart full as the two kissed.

As the stars began to dot the sky, the group gathered around a fire pit near the barn, their laughter and conversation mingling with the crackle of the flames. Daniel sat beside Maggie, his arm wrapped around her shoulders, while Pete and Clara shared quiet smiles from across the fire. Even Bear lay contentedly by the fire, his head resting on his paws as the soft glow reflected in his dark eyes. The wedding plans became the center of attention once more, with Maggie excitedly sharing her vision for the ceremony.

"I want it to be simple, just like us," she said, her eyes sparkling as she looked at Daniel. "The oak tree by the pond is the perfect spot, and Clara will help with the decorations."

Clara beamed at the mention of her name. "I've already started thinking about flowers and lanterns. We can string them from the branches, and I'll make sure everything is perfect."

Pete chimed in with a grin. "I'll take care of the benches. And don't worry, Daniel, I'll make sure the barn is ready for the reception."

Daniel laughed, squeezing Maggie's hand. "Sounds like we've got ourselves a real team here."

The mood was light. The fire's warmth and the company's joy made the world's troubles seem distant, if only for the moment. As the evening wore on and the fire began to die, Daniel and Maggie stood by the paddock, watching Willow graze quietly in the moonlight. Maggie leaned her head against Daniel's shoulder, her heart full as she thought about the future they were building together.

"I can't believe how far we've come," Maggie whispered, her voice soft. "A few months ago, everything felt so uncertain, and now... we're planning a wedding.

We've got Pete and Clara. It feels like everything is falling into place." Daniel kissed the top of her head, his arm tightening around her. "We've been through a lot, but we've made it. And now, we're building something even better. Something worth fighting for."

Maggie smiled, lifting her gaze to meet his. "I'm ready for whatever comes next as long as I'm with you."

Daniel's eyes shone with love as he leaned down and kissed her, the stars above them twinkling like future promises. Bear padded over to them, wagging his tail and nuzzling Maggie's hand as if reminding them they were never alone. As they stood together in the stillness of the night, the weight of the past seemed to fade, leaving only the hope of the future and the promise of the love they had fought so hard to protect.

Chapter Thirty-One: Shadows of the Past

The moon hung high over Whitaker Farm, casting long shadows across the fields as a cool breeze whispered through the trees. The peace of the evening was deceptive, masking the tension that had begun to build. After the sheriff's warning about Jonathan Townsend, the air felt thick with a quiet dread, a storm waiting to break. Daniel could feel it in his bones. Maggie stood by the window inside the farmhouse, her arms wrapped tightly around herself. The stillness of the night did little to calm the knot of anxiety in her chest. She tried to focus on the upcoming wedding and the life she and Daniel were building together, but her thoughts kept circling back to the threat looming over them.

"Daniel?" she called softly, her voice carrying a note of unease.

Daniel appeared from the kitchen, his brow creased with concern. He had felt it, too—an unsettling energy hanging in the air.

"I was just about to check the barn. Something doesn't feel right tonight."

Maggie's heart fluttered with nerves. "I feel it, too."

Before Daniel could respond, a deep, guttural bark split the silence—Bear, standing near the barn, barking at something in the distance. The urgency in his voice sent a chill through both of them.

Daniel grabbed his rifle without hesitation and rushed to the door, with Maggie close behind. As they stepped outside, a cool wind swept across the yard, and in the distance, they could hear the unmistakable sound of hooves pounding the dirt path. A rider was approaching fast.

"Stay behind me," Daniel ordered, his voice tense.

Bear barked again, his body stiff as he paced the fence, his eyes locked on the dark figure galloping toward them. The faint silhouette of a rider emerged from the shadows, and as he drew closer, the moonlight revealed the familiar features of a man they had hoped never to see again. Jonathan Townsend. Daniel's grip on the rifle tightened as Jonathan slowed his horse to a stop just beyond the fence. His dark eyes gleamed with malice as he dismounted, his boots crunching against the gravel with each heavy step. The wind tugged at his coat, making him look more menacing as he stood there, facing them.

"I warned you, Whitaker," Jonathan called, his voice carrying across the yard with a dangerous edge. "I told you there'd be consequences for my brother's death."

Maggie felt her heart race as Jonathan's words hung in the air. Edward Townsend had been dangerous enough in life, but Jonathan was more unpredictable—driven by vengeance and a sense of entitlement that made him even more volatile. Daniel stepped forward, positioning himself protectively in front of Maggie.

"Your brother made his own choices, and he paid for them. You don't get to come here and stir up trouble, Jonathan."

Jonathan sneered, his hand resting on the revolver strapped to his side. "Trouble? You haven't seen trouble yet. I'm here to settle the score, and I don't care what I have to do to make sure you pay for what happened to Edward."

The tension in the air was suffocating, thick with the promise of violence. Bear growled low in his throat, his eyes never leaving Jonathan as if sensing the danger in his every move.

"You think you can come onto my land and threaten us?" Daniel's voice was low and steady, though his grip on the rifle betrayed his readiness for a fight. "You're not leaving here with the upper hand, Jonathan. Not this time."

Just as the standoff between Daniel and Jonathan reached its breaking point, the sound of galloping hooves broke the tense silence. Clara and Pete appeared at the edge of the yard, their faces etched with concern. They had been out by the orchard when they heard Bear's frantic barking and had rushed over, sensing something was wrong.

"What's going on?" Pete called out as he and Clara dismounted quickly, their eyes scanning the tense scene.

"Jonathan," Daniel replied, his voice tight with anger. "He's here to stir up trouble."

Jonathan's gaze flicked to Clara and Pete as they approached, his expression twisted with contempt.

"You think you can all stand against me? My family's been in this town for generations. You don't know the kind of power we have."

Clara felt a chill run down her spine as Jonathan's words hung in the air. She had heard stories about the Townsend family, their wealth and influence spreading far beyond Briarwood, but she had never encountered their wrath firsthand—until now. Pete clenched his fists, stepping forward to stand beside Daniel. His voice was steady, though anger simmered beneath the surface.

"Maybe your family has power, but that doesn't give you the right to come here and threaten us. This is Daniel's and Maggie's home, and we won't let you tear it apart."

Jonathan's sneer deepened, and in that moment, something dark flashed in his eyes. "You're all fools if you think you can stop me."

Without warning, Jonathan drew his revolver, the cold metal glinting in the moonlight as he pointed it directly at Daniel. Maggie gasped, her heart slamming against her chest as time seemed to slow. The world around her blurred, her focus narrowing to the man standing just feet away, ready to pull the trigger.

The crack of the gunshot split the night, echoing across the fields. For a moment, everything stood still. Maggie's breath caught in her throat, her eyes wide as she watched Jonathan stagger back, his revolver clattering to the ground. Blood seeped through his fingers as he clutched his shoulder, his expression one of disbelief as he collapsed to the dirt.

Daniel stood his ground, his rifle still raised, the barrel smoking from the shot. His breathing was heavy, his eyes locked on Jonathan, but he didn't move. He didn't need to. The danger had passed, but the weight of what had just happened hung in the air. Pete rushed forward, kneeling beside Jonathan to check his injury.

"He's alive," Pete called out, though his tone was grim. "But we need to get him to the doctor."

Clara stepped forward, her face pale but determined. "I'll help. We need to get him into town before he loses too much blood."

Maggie's legs felt weak, her hands trembling as she clutched Daniel's arm. The adrenaline coursing through her veins made her feel light-headed, but she couldn't tear her eyes away from Jonathan, lying wounded on the ground. She couldn't believe how close they had come to disaster.

"You saved us," she whispered, her voice trembling as she looked up at Daniel, her eyes filled with gratitude and shock.

Daniel finally lowered his rifle, his gaze softening as he turned to her. "I wasn't going to let him hurt you, Maggie. Not ever."

With Jonathan taken care of and the immediate danger over, the night began to quiet once more. Pete and Clara had ridden off to town with Jonathan, leaving Daniel and Maggie alone on the farm, the moonlight casting a soft glow over the fields. Maggie sat on the porch, her legs still shaky from the night's events.

Daniel sat beside her, wrapping an arm around her shoulders as she leaned into him. The warmth of his presence grounded her, calming the whirlwind of emotions swirling inside her.

"You could have been killed," Maggie said softly, her voice breaking slightly as she recalled the moment Jonathan pulled the gun.

Daniel pressed a kiss to her temple, his hand resting on hers. "But I wasn't. And neither were you. That's all that matters."

Maggie closed her eyes, her heart aching with love for the man beside her. "I don't know what I would have done if… if something had happened to you." Daniel turned to face her, his gaze filled with tenderness.

"You don't have to think about that, Maggie. We're here together. And I'm not going anywhere."

Their eyes met, and in that moment, the weight of the night seemed to lift. Maggie leaned in, her lips meeting his in a slow, lingering kiss that spoke of the love they had fought so hard to protect. The world around them faded, leaving only the two under the starry sky, their hearts beating as one. When they finally pulled apart, Daniel rested his forehead against hers, his voice low and filled with emotion.

"No matter what happens, I'll always protect you. We've been through so much, but we've got a future to look forward to. And nothing's going to take that away from us."

Maggie smiled, her heart swelling with love as she whispered, "I believe you. I love you, Daniel."

As they sat together under the stars, Bear padded over and rested his head on Maggie's lap, a soft whine escaping him as if he had also sensed the danger.

Maggie laughed softly, scratching Bear behind the ears, the tension finally leaving her body. With Jonathan gone, the future felt brighter than it had in a long time. They had faced the shadows of the past, and together, they would face whatever came next—stronger, braver, and filled with love.

Chapter Thirty-Two: Ripples in Briarwood

Whitaker Farm was quiet the morning after the confrontation with Jonathan Townsend, but the previous night's unease lingered. Maggie stood on the porch, watching the sun slowly rise over the fields, casting a golden light across the land. It should have been a peaceful scene, but her thoughts were clouded with worry. Daniel joined her, his expression grim as he gazed at the horizon.

"I'm heading into town later," he said quietly. "I need to talk to Sheriff Turner and make sure there won't be any trouble from the Townsends."

Maggie's heart sank. "Do you think Jonathan will press charges?"

Daniel sighed, running a hand through his hair. "If he doesn't, his family will. They won't let this go, Maggie. Not without a fight."

Maggie reached for his hand, squeezing it gently. "We'll get through this. We've faced worse."

Daniel gave her a small, tired smile. "You're right. But it feels like the town's turning into a powder keg, just waiting for someone to light the fuse."

Later that morning, Daniel rode into Briarwood. As he passed through the town's center, he couldn't help but notice how people looked at him. Some nodded in quiet approval, but others whispered behind his back, their eyes filled with suspicion.

The story of Jonathan's injury spread fast, and everyone seemed to have an opinion. Daniel tied his horse to the post outside Sheriff Turner's office and stepped inside, deep in thought, finding the sheriff at his desk.

He looked up, his expression grim as he motioned for Daniel to sit. "We've got a situation on our hands," Sheriff said, his voice low. "Jonathan's family is pushing hard for legal action. They're claiming you shot him in cold blood."

Daniel clenched his jaw. "He pulled a gun on me, Sheriff. I was defending myself and Maggie."

"I know that," Sheriff Turner replied, leaning back in his chair. "But the Townsends are powerful and have people in their pocket. It's going to be a battle, Daniel."

Daniel's fists tightened. "So, what do we do?"

Turner sighed. "For now, we keep things calm. Don't stir up any more trouble. The last thing we need is a full-blown feud breaking out in town. I'll do what I can to keep the law on your side, but be prepared. This could get ugly."

As Daniel left the sheriff's office, he felt the weight of the town's eyes on him. The tension in the air was palpable, like a storm waiting to break. And the storm had a name—Townsend.

Back at the farm, Maggie was busy preparing for the wedding, trying to distract herself from the growing tension. Clara and Pete were there to help, working alongside her to set up decorations and plan the final details. As they worked in the barn, stringing lanterns and arranging flowers, Maggie noticed the quiet smiles and lingering glances between Clara and Pete. It warmed her heart to see their bond growing stronger, even in the midst of everything else.

"Clara, what do you think about the arch over there?" Maggie asked, gesturing toward the spot where she and Daniel planned to exchange vows.

Clara smiled, her blue eyes bright with excitement. "It'll be perfect. I can't wait to see it all come together."

Pete walked over, his hands dusty from moving wooden beams. "I'll make sure everything's ready in time. Nothing's stopping this wedding from being perfect."

Clara looked up at him, her smile softening. "You've been working so hard, Pete. I don't know how we'd do it without you."

Pete shrugged, but his gaze lingered on Clara a little longer than necessary. "I'm happy to do it. For you and Maggie."

As they continued to work, Clara and Pete's closeness became more apparent. When their hands brushed as they reached for the same flower arrangement, Clara blushed, and Pete grinned, his eyes filled with affection. It was clear that something deeper was growing between them.

As the afternoon wore on, Daniel returned from town, his expression grim as he told Maggie about the situation with the Townsends.

"We'll have to be on our guard," he said quietly. "They're not going to back down easily."

Maggie nodded, her heart heavy. "We'll get through this. Together."

But that night, something unexpected happened as the farm settled into its usual quiet. Bear began barking furiously from the paddock, his sharp barks cutting through the stillness of the night. Maggie and Daniel rushed outside, their hearts pounding with alarm.

"What is it, boy?" Daniel called, following Bear's lead as the dog barked at something near the fence.

In the dim moonlight, Daniel spotted something glinting in the grass. He knelt down and picked it up—a piece of paper, crumpled and damp from the evening dew. As he unfolded it, his blood ran cold.

It was a note, scrawled in harsh, angry handwriting: "You're not safe. We'll make sure of that."

Maggie gasped, her hand flying to her mouth as she read the words over Daniel's shoulder.

"Who would do this?"

Daniel's face hardened. "It's them. The Townsends."

"We need to tell the sheriff," Maggie said, trembling. "This is a threat, Daniel."

Daniel nodded, crumpling the note in his hand. "We will. But we can't rely on the law alone. We need to protect ourselves."

Daniel and Maggie shared a quiet moment that evening despite the fear gripping them. After ensuring the farm was secure, they sat on the porch, wrapped in a blanket under the stars. Maggie leaned against Daniel, feeling the steady beat of his heart.

"No matter what happens, I'm glad we have each other," she whispered.

Daniel wrapped his arm around her, pressing a kiss to the top of her head. "I love you, Maggie. And nothing—not the Townsends or anyone else—is going to change that."

Maggie smiled, her heart swelling with love. "We've been through so much already. I know we'll get through this too."

Daniel kissed her, slow and deep, his hands cradling her face as if she were the most precious thing in the world. In that moment, the outside world fell away, leaving only the two of them and the love that had grown stronger each day. As they pulled back, Daniel rested his forehead against hers, his voice low and filled with emotion. "We'll face this together. Just like we always have."

Maggie nodded, her eyes shining with love. "Always."

The next few days were a whirlwind of wedding preparations, but the tension from the Townsends' threats hung in the air. Clara and Pete continued to work closely together, their bond growing stronger with each passing day. Pete, emboldened by everything they had been through, finally found the courage to express his feelings to Clara. Clara sat by the barn, her arms wrapped around her knees as she watched the sky shift from vibrant oranges to soft purples.

She was lost in thought, her heart filled with the emotions that had been building between her and Pete over the last few weeks. Pete, who had been finishing up with the horses, spotted her sitting alone and felt his heart quicken. He knew that now was the moment—after all they had been through, it was time to say what had been on his mind for so long. He walked over to her, his steps slow and deliberate, as if he were savoring the moment. Clara looked up as Pete approached, a soft smile playing on her lips.

"It's beautiful, isn't it?" she asked, gesturing to the fading sunset.

Pete nodded, sitting down beside her. "Yeah," he agreed, though his gaze was fixed on her, not the horizon. "It's more beautiful with you here."

Clara's cheeks flushed at his words, and she looked down for a moment, her heart fluttering. There had been so many moments like this between them—small, quiet exchanges that spoke of something deeper, something neither of them had dared to fully express. But tonight was different. Pete reached out, gently taking her hand in his. His thumb brushed over her knuckles as he turned to face her, his voice soft but full of emotion.

"Clara, I don't want to wait any longer to say this. I love you. I've known it for a while now, but I needed to make sure I said it right."

Clara's breath caught in her throat as she looked into his eyes, the sincerity and love in his gaze overwhelming her. Her heart swelled with the same feeling—something she had known deep down but hadn't yet spoken aloud.

"I love you too, Pete," she whispered, her voice trembling. "I've felt it for so long, and I can't imagine my life without you."

The words hung between them briefly, their hearts pounding in unison as the full weight of their confession settled over them.

Then, without hesitation, Pete leaned in, closing the small distance between them. His lips brushed against hers in a soft, tender kiss that spoke of everything they had shared—of every quiet moment, every unspoken feeling. Clara's eyes fluttered closed as she kissed him back, her heart racing with the realization that this was real—that the love they had both felt was finally out in the open.

When they pulled apart, their foreheads rested against each other, their breath mingling in the cool evening air.

"I've been waiting to say that," Pete murmured, his voice filled with quiet joy. "And now that I have, I never want to stop saying it."

Clara smiled, her heart full. "Neither do I."

They sat together as the sun's last light disappeared, holding each other close as the stars began to appear in the sky. In that moment, everything felt right—like the beginning of something beautiful, something lasting.

Chapter Thirty-Three: Flames and Favors

The days leading up to the wedding had been a whirlwind of preparation. The farmhouse was a hub of activity, with Maggie, Clara, Daniel, and Pete working tirelessly to ensure everything was perfect. Yet, despite the joy that should have filled the air, there was a weight of unease that none could shake.

The Townsend family's threats had not been idle, and Maggie couldn't help but feel like a shadow was looming over her happiest day. Maggie tried to focus on the wedding preparations. The bouquets of wildflowers Clara had picked were already arranged, and the lanterns Daniel had hung around the barn glowed softly as the evening settled in. But Maggie's heart was heavy, and the anxious knot in her stomach never seemed to ease.

"I keep thinking about what else they might do," Maggie admitted to Clara as they worked together, tying ribbons onto the chairs set out for the guests. "I know the wedding should be all I'm thinking about, but I can't help it."

Clara paused, her hands gentle as she adjusted a ribbon. "You've been through so much, Maggie. It's no wonder you're worried. But you have to remember—you're not alone in this. We're all here for you. And we'll get through whatever comes our way."

Maggie smiled weakly, appreciating Clara's words, but the underlying tension in her chest didn't ease. Something was unsettling in the air, growing heavier with each passing moment.

Later that evening, the farmhouse had finally settled into a comfortable quiet. Daniel and Maggie sat together by the fire, enjoying the warmth of the flames. Bear lay at their feet, his head resting lazily on his paws, while Willow grazed peacefully outside the barn. The evening was still, but the unease growing all day was now a palpable tension in the air. Suddenly, Bear's ears perked up, his head snapping toward the barn. Without warning, he bolted to his feet, barking furiously. The deep, echoing barks shattered the calm of the night, sending a jolt of fear through Maggie's chest.

"What's wrong, boy?" Daniel asked, standing up and grabbing the lantern from the mantle.

Bear's barking grew more frantic as he ran toward the barn, his tail stiff, his body tense. Maggie and Daniel exchanged a worried glance before rushing outside, the cold evening air biting against their skin. As they approached the barn, the smell of smoke, sharp and acrid, hit them. Maggie's heart stopped in her chest as her eyes widened in horror.

Flames were licking up the side of the barn, orange and red tendrils dancing against the wood, spreading faster than they could comprehend.

"Oh no…" Maggie gasped, her voice trembling as she instinctively reached for Daniel's hand. "The barn!"

Daniel's jaw clenched, his eyes narrowing as the gravity of the situation sank in. "Someone set this. Get Willow out—now!"

Maggie nodded, running toward the paddock where Willow was stamping nervously, her ears pinned back in fear. The mare whinnied anxiously as Maggie reached her, her hands trembling as she untied the reins and led her away from the barn.

"Come on, girl, you're safe now." Meanwhile, Daniel rushed into the barn, coughing against the smoke as he quickly unlatched the stalls for the other animals, guiding them out to safety. The flames crackled loudly, growing higher, the heat becoming unbearable as they battled against time.

Just as Daniel emerged from the barn with the last animals, Pete, Hank, and Clara appeared, running toward them with wide eyes, their faces pale in the firelight.

"Hank, get more water!" Pete shouted, as Hank nodded and rushed to the well, grabbing buckets.

"What happened?" Clara cried, looking between Maggie and Daniel.

"It's them," Daniel replied grimly, his voice tight with fury. "The Townsends."

Hank returned with buckets in hand and passed one to Pete and Clara. As the fire continued to spread, Hank, Pete, and Daniel threw water on the flames, desperately trying to slow its advance. Sam, who had healed tremendously, also arrived, breathless and determined. The group worked frantically together, though the flames were quickly overtaking their efforts. Just when it seemed like the fire would consume the entire barn, a distant shout caught Maggie's attention.

She turned to see a group of riders galloping toward the farm, their faces lit by the glow of the fire. Sheriff Turner led the charge, his face grim with determination, and behind him rode a dozen townspeople, armed with buckets, shovels, and anything else they could use to fight the blaze.

"We came as soon as we saw the smoke!" the sheriff shouted as he leaped from his horse, grabbing a bucket and joining the efforts to control the fire. The townspeople worked together with Daniel, Pete, Hank, Sam, Clara, and Maggie, and their collective efforts finally started to make a difference. The flames, once roaring, were now being beaten back as water was thrown at them from all sides. Slowly but surely, the fire began to die down. Maggie stood with Clara, arms around each other as they watched the townspeople rally around them. It was an overwhelming sight—people they had known their whole lives coming to their rescue in their darkest hour. The tension in Maggie's chest loosened slightly as she realized they weren't fighting this battle alone.

"I can't believe they came," Maggie whispered, her voice choked with emotion.

Clara smiled, her eyes misty. "They love you, Maggie. You and Daniel. This town sticks together."

As the last of the flames were doused, Mr. Hargrove, a long-time resident of Briarwood, approached Maggie and Daniel. His face was lined with age, but his eyes were kind and steady.

"You two don't need to worry," he said in his low, gravelly voice. "We won't let those Townsends take anything from you. This town's got your back."

Daniel nodded, his voice thick with gratitude. "Thank you, Mr. Hargrove. We couldn't have saved the barn without you."

The older man gave a small smile, tipping his hat. "We take care of our own, son. Don't ever forget that."

As the townspeople began to leave, promising to return the next day to help repair the barn, a lone rider appeared in the distance. The air had cooled considerably, and the night was now calm after the chaos, but the sight of the unknown rider brought a new wave of tension. The rider dismounted just beyond the fence, his boots crunching against the dirt as he walked toward them. The dim glow of the remaining lanterns illuminated his dark hair and sharp features. His clothes were worn but of fine quality, suggesting a man of some means.

"Daniel Whitaker?" the man called out, his voice low and steady. Daniel stepped forward, his protective instinct immediately kicking in.

"That's me. Who are you?" The man removed his hat, nodding slightly in respect. "I'm Samuel Pierce. I worked with your father many years ago. I've come to offer my help."

Maggie frowned, confusion swirling in her mind. She glanced at Daniel, who looked equally wary.

"I've never heard of you before," Daniel said, his tone cautious. "What kind of help are you offering?"

Samuel stepped closer, his eyes flicking toward the barn before settling back on Daniel. "I've been hearing things—about the Townsend family. About their dealings with dangerous people. I know how they operate and won't stop until they've taken everything from you. But I can help."

Daniel crossed his arms, his jaw tight. "Why should we trust you?" Samuel met Daniel's gaze without hesitation. "Because I know the Townsends better than anyone. They've been involved in more than just local disputes—they're tied to larger players, and those players are dangerous. You're caught in something bigger than you realize."

Maggie's heart pounded in her chest as she listened to Samuel's words. The weight of what he was saying settled over her like a heavy cloak. This wasn't just about revenge or family pride anymore—it was about survival.

"We'll talk," Daniel said finally, his voice low and filled with determination. "But know this—we'll protect what's ours. The Townsends won't get away with this."

As the night deepened and the last of the townspeople rode away, Maggie and Daniel stood together in the quiet of the night. The barn had been saved, but the tension lingered like smoke in the air. Maggie leaned against Daniel, her heart still racing from the night's events, while Bear paced restlessly by their side. The smell of smoke still hung in the air, mixing with the cool evening breeze. She closed her eyes, listening to the sounds of the night—the distant calls of owls, the soft rustling of the trees—but none of it was enough to quiet the fear that gnawed at the edges of her thoughts.

"Do you think we can trust him?" she asked, her voice barely above a whisper.

The weight of Samuel Pierce's arrival and his cryptic warnings still loomed heavily over her. Daniel was silent momentarily, his arm wrapped around Maggie's shoulders as they both stared out at the farm—the place they had fought so hard to protect. He was calm on the surface, but Maggie could feel the tension in his body, the way his muscles tightened beneath his shirt.

"I don't know," Daniel admitted, his voice thick with uncertainty. "But if what he says is true, then we might be deeper than we thought. We'll have to be careful."

Maggie nodded, the unease still twisting inside her. She tried to focus on the positive—the fact that they had saved the barn, that the townspeople had rallied around them—but it was hard to shake the fear of what might come next.

"We've faced everything together so far," she said softly, trying to reassure both Daniel and herself. "We'll get through this too."

Daniel kissed the top of her head, his voice low and full of conviction. "I won't let anyone take this from us. Not the Townsends, not anyone. We've built too much and fought too hard. I'll do whatever it takes to keep you safe, Maggie."

The intensity in his voice comforted Maggie's heart, even though the future felt uncertain. She rested her head on his chest, letting the steady beat of his heart soothe her.

The next morning, the farm was alive with activity again, but this time, it wasn't just the usual bustle of wedding preparations. The townspeople had returned, just as they had promised, ready to help rebuild what had been damaged. Hank and Sam were already working hard, hauling wood and coordinating repairs.

Hammers rang out, wood was hauled, and voices filled the air with a sense of community and solidarity that lifted everyone's spirits. Maggie stood on the porch, watching as Mr. Hargrove, Sheriff Turner, and other familiar faces worked together to repair the barn. It was a sight that warmed her heart, a reminder that despite the danger they faced, they were not alone.

"We'll have this barn fixed in no time," Mr. Hargrove called out with a grin, wiping the sweat from his brow. "You'll have the place looking even better than it was before."

Maggie smiled, her heart swelling with gratitude. "Thank you, Mr. Hargrove. We couldn't have done this without all of you."

The older man chuckled, waving her off. "It's what neighbors do. We look out for each other. You and Daniel are a part of this town, and we're not about to let the Townsends drive you away."

As Maggie turned back toward the house, she saw Clara and Pete working side by side, their faces bright with the joy of being together. Their hands brushed as they passed tools back and forth, and Maggie couldn't help but smile at the blossoming love between them. Clara caught her eye and waved.

"We're almost done with this part! Pete's been incredible—he's practically rebuilt half the barn on his own!"

Pete laughed, shaking his head. "I just want to make sure it's solid. After all, it's got to stand through your wedding, right?"

Maggie's heart warmed at their playful banter. Despite everything, there was still so much love and hope around her. Even with the looming threat of the Townsends, the bond between them all was unbreakable.

As the day wore on and the sun began to dip low in the sky, Maggie and Daniel found a quiet moment alone, sitting together by the old oak tree near the pond.

The wedding was just days away, but there was still so much left to do. And now, with the appearance of Samuel Pierce and the ever-present threat of the Townsend family, it was hard to focus on the joy of the upcoming ceremony.

"I wish we could just… enjoy this," Maggie said softly, leaning against Daniel's shoulder. "I want to think about the wedding, about our future together, but it feels like there's a storm on the horizon."

Daniel wrapped his arm around her, his thumb tracing small circles on her arm.

"I know," he said quietly. "But we can't let them take this from us, Maggie. We can't let them take away what we've built, what we're about to start together."

Maggie sighed, her heart heavy with the weight of it all. "Do you think Samuel was right? About the Townsends being tied to dangerous people?"

Daniel was silent for a long moment before nodding. "I think there's a lot more going on than we know. And if Samuel's right, then we will have to be careful. But I believe him when he says he wants to help."

Maggie looked up at him, her eyes filled with worry. "What if he's part of the danger? What if trusting him is a mistake?"

Daniel's expression softened, and he cupped her cheek, brushing his thumb gently across her skin. "We'll be smart about it. I won't let anyone hurt you, Maggie. No matter what."

His words brought a sense of calm to her, a reminder of their shared strength. Together, they had faced so much; together, they would face whatever came next. But for now, as the sun set behind the trees and the day drew to a close, Maggie allowed herself to breathe and focus on the love surrounding her. The future was uncertain, but she knew one thing for sure—she had Daniel by her side, and together, they would weather any storm.

Chapter Thirty-Four: The Calm and the Storm

The next morning dawned with the smell of fresh dew and the sounds of hammers still ringing in the air as Sam, Hank, and Pete worked tirelessly to repair the damage from the fire. The sun was warm on their backs, but the tension from the previous night lingered like a stubborn cloud, casting shadows over their minds. Daniel stood nearby, overseeing the work with pride and unease. His farmhands were good men—loyal, hard-working, and trustworthy—but after the sabotage, the sense that something worse might be coming gnawed at him. He couldn't shake the feeling that the Townsend family was planning more than fires.

"How's it looking?" Daniel asked as he approached Pete, who was nailing new planks onto the barn wall. Pete wiped the sweat from his brow and nodded.

"We'll have this patched up by the end of the day. Sam and Hank have been working like madmen—if there's another fire, I reckon this barn will stand up to it better than before."

Daniel gave a half-smile though his mind was elsewhere. "Good. But let's hope there's no need for it."

Inside the farmhouse, Maggie and Clara were busy with last-minute wedding preparations. Willow grazed lazily outside, occasionally sticking her head through the open window to nuzzle Maggie's arm as if sensing her unease. Maggie couldn't help but smile, rubbing Willow's nose affectionately, though her thoughts were still swirling with worries about the wedding and the threats hanging over them.

"What are you thinking about?" Clara asked, glancing up from where she was arranging flowers on the kitchen table.

Maggie sighed, her fingers lingering on the lace of her wedding dress that lay draped over a nearby chair. "I'm just... trying to picture the wedding without something going wrong. I wonder if we should postpone it until things settle down with the Townsends."

Clara's expression softened. "Maggie, you deserve this happiness. You and Daniel both do. The whole town is behind you. No matter what the Townsends try, you'll have us all standing with you."

Maggie nodded, but the weight of the threats still sat heavy on her heart. "I just want it to be perfect."

Clara reached out and took Maggie's hand. "It will be. And if anything happens, we'll face it together, like we always do."

Later that afternoon, as the repairs were nearly finished, Daniel called Sam, Hank, and Pete over to the farmhouse porch. Sheriff Turner had stopped by, leaning against the porch railing with his arms crossed, surveying the farm.

"We've done the repairs," Daniel said, his voice steady but firm. "But we need to be prepared for whatever the Townsends might throw at us next. The fire was just the beginning."

Pete nodded, his face serious. "What do you want us to do, boss?"

Daniel glanced at the sheriff, then back to his farmhands. "I want the farm guarded—around the clock. We'll take shifts. If they try anything else, we'll be ready. Hank, you'll take the first watch tonight."

Hank's brow furrowed, but he nodded. "You got it. Ain't no Townsend gonna sneak onto this land again without me knowing."

The sheriff chimed in, his voice calm but resolute. "I'll have a deputy keep an eye on things in town, too. The Townsends have a long reach, but they're not invincible. We'll make sure this doesn't escalate any further."

Sam, who had been quiet for most of the meeting, spoke up, his voice steady. "If it comes down to it, we won't let them hurt anyone. This farm is our home, too. We'll stand by you, Daniel."

Daniel nodded, appreciating the loyalty of his men. "We'll stand together. All of us." That evening, as the sun set over the farm, casting a golden glow across the fields, Maggie and Daniel found a quiet moment together under the oak tree by the pond. The worries of the day had been set aside, if only for a little while, and they sat in the warm, fading light, their hands intertwined.

"It feels like everything's changing," Maggie said softly, leaning her head against Daniel's shoulder. "The wedding, the Townsends, the fire… I feel like we're on the edge of something."

Daniel squeezed her hand gently. "We are. But whatever happens, we'll face it together. You and me." Maggie looked up at him, her blue eyes filled with love and determination.

"I don't want to be afraid anymore, Daniel. I just want to think about us— our future." Daniel's expression softened, and he leaned down, brushing his lips against hers in a tender kiss.

"We'll have that future, Maggie. No one's going to take it from us."

They sat in silence for a while, watching as the stars began to appear in the darkening sky, the soft sounds of the farm around them. The threats from the Townsends still loomed, but in that moment, surrounded by the love and support of their community, Maggie felt a sense of peace she hadn't felt in days.

As the night deepened, Hank took up his position near the barn, a rifle slung over his shoulder, his eyes scanning the horizon for any sign of movement. Bear lay at his feet, ears perked and alert. The night was quiet, save for the occasional rustle of leaves in the breeze. Meanwhile, Sam and Pete worked quietly on reinforcing the gates and fences, ensuring that no one could slip onto the property unnoticed. The tension was thick in the air, but there was also a sense of purpose—a determination to protect what mattered most.

As the night wore on, Hank glanced toward the farmhouse, where a single lantern flickered in the window. He couldn't see inside, but he knew that Maggie and Daniel were together, and that was all that mattered.

"We'll keep them safe," Hank muttered to himself, his grip tightening on his rifle. "No one's getting past us tonight."

Just as the moon climbed high in the sky, Bear's ears shot up, and he growled low in his throat. Hank tensed, scanning the tree line. The shadows seemed to shift, and for a moment, Hank thought he saw movement—something or someone lurking just beyond the edge of the woods.

"Hank?" Pete's voice whispered from nearby, his silhouette barely visible in the darkness. "You see something?"

"I'm not sure," Hank replied, his voice low. "But stay alert. I've got a bad feeling." Bear's growl deepened, his body low to the ground as he watched the treeline. Whatever was out there, it was close.

Chapter Thirty-Five: Lurking Shadows

The stillness of the night had taken on a dangerous edge. Hank stood motionless, his eyes fixed on the shifting shadows beyond the tree line. Bear growled softly, his ears perked, his body coiled like a spring, ready to pounce at the slightest sign of danger. The farm had become a fortress, yet the presence in the woods made it clear—they were being watched. Pete slowly moved closer from his post near the fence to Hank, his voice a low whisper.

"Do you think it's them?"

Hank's grip tightened on his rifle. "Could be. It could be somethin' else. But I ain't takin' no chances."

For a few tense minutes, the only sound was the rustling of the wind through the trees. Then, suddenly, there was a distinct crack—a branch snapping underfoot. Bear lunged forward, barking ferociously as he darted toward the source of the noise.

Hank raised his rifle, his heart pounding. "Show yourself!" he shouted, his voice carrying through the stillness of the night.

A figure emerged from the trees, stumbling into the moonlight. For a split second, Hank and Pete braced for the worst, but as the figure came closer, the tension eased slightly—it wasn't just one of the Townsends. It was Jonathan Townsend's younger brother, Nathan.

Nathan was younger, thinner, and far less imposing than his brothers, but there was a familiar sneer on his face as he stepped forward. His clothes were disheveled, and his eyes had a wild look to them, as if he hadn't slept in days.

"What are you doin' out here?" Hank demanded, keeping his rifle aimed at Nathan.

Pete, standing nearby, tightened his grip on his own weapon, ready for anything.

Nathan smirked, though there was something desperate in his eyes. "Just checking on the family's investment, Hank. You and Pete sure are jumpy for a couple of farmhands."

"You call settin' fire to the barn checkin' on your investment?" Pete growled, his voice low and dangerous. "You've got a lot of nerve, showin' up here after what your family's done."

Nathan raised his hands in mock surrender, though the sneer never left his face. "Now, now. I'm not here to cause trouble. In fact, I've got a proposition for Daniel."

Hank narrowed his eyes. "You ain't gonna talk to Daniel. You got somethin' to say, you can tell it to us."

Nathan's expression darkened, and for a moment, the sneer faltered. "My brothers—they've gone too far," he said quietly. "I didn't want any part of this. But things are happening… things you don't know about. If you're smart, you'll take my offer to Daniel."

Pete stepped forward, his eyes flashing with anger. "We ain't interested in any offer you've got. If you think you can threaten us into—"

"It's not a threat," Nathan interrupted, his voice sharp. "It's a warning." Nathan's words hung in the air, thick with an unspoken danger. For a moment, the only sound was the distant rustling of the trees, as if the woods themselves were holding their breath.

"What kind of warning?" Hank asked, lowering his rifle slightly, though his posture remained tense. Nathan glanced around, his eyes flicking nervously toward the farmhouse, as if expecting someone to be watching him.

"There's more at play here than just my brothers and your little farm. They've made deals… dangerous deals. And if you don't take this seriously, things are going to get worse—much worse."

Pete's jaw clenched, his hands curling into fists. "And what's your offer? We back down and let your family run this town?"

Nathan shook his head, stepping closer, his voice dropping to a conspiratorial whisper. "No. I'm offering you a way out. A way to stop this before it spirals out of control. But you need to talk to Daniel—now, before it's too late."

Hank exchanged a glance with Pete, his gut telling him that there was more to Nathan's visit than just empty threats. But there was no way he was letting Nathan anywhere near Daniel without a fight.

"You ain't seein' Daniel," Hank said firmly. "We'll pass your message along. Now get out of here before we change our minds."

Nathan's lips curled into a twisted smile. "Fine. But don't say I didn't warn you."

With that, he turned and disappeared back into the woods, leaving Hank and Pete standing in the moonlight, their minds racing with questions.

Back at the farmhouse, Maggie and Daniel were in the kitchen, the soft glow of the lanterns casting long shadows across the room. Maggie had been trying to distract herself with wedding plans, but the tension from the day weighed heavily on her.

"Do you think they'll try something else?" Maggie asked, her voice barely above a whisper. Daniel didn't respond right away, his jaw tight as he stared out the window, his thoughts far away.

"I don't know," he said finally. "But whatever they're planning, we'll be ready."

Just as the words left his mouth, the front door swung open, and Hank and Pete entered, their faces grim. Maggie's heart skipped a beat as she saw the look in their eyes—something had happened.

"What is it?" Daniel asked, his voice sharp and concerned.

Hank stepped forward, his expression dark. "We just had ourselves a visitor—Nathan Townsend."

Maggie's breath caught in her throat. "What did he want?"

"He says he's not here to cause trouble," Pete replied, though the disbelief in his voice was clear. "Says he's got a warning for you."

Daniel's brow furrowed. "What kind of warning?"

Hank shook his head. "Somethin' about his brothers making deals with dangerous people. He's sayin' things are gonna get worse if we don't do somethin'."

Daniel's expression hardened, and Maggie felt a chill run down her spine. She knew the Townsends were trouble, but this was something different—something darker.

"What do you think?" Maggie asked quietly, her voice trembling slightly. "Do we trust him?"

Daniel was silent for a long moment, his eyes dark and unreadable. "I don't know," he said finally. "But if Nathan's telling the truth, then we're in deeper than we thought."

As the night deepened, Daniel, Maggie, Hank, Pete, and Sam gathered around the table, discussing their next move. The warning from Nathan had left them all on edge, but there was no clear path forward.

"We need to be smart about this," Daniel said, his voice calm but firm. "If Nathan's right, then the Townsends aren't just after the farm—they're after something bigger."

Sam, who had been quiet throughout most of the conversation, finally spoke up. "If it's true, then we need to get ahead of this. Find out who they're dealing with and cut them off before things get out of hand."

Pete nodded in agreement. "We can't wait for them to make the next move. We've gotta be ready." Maggie looked around the table, her heart heavy with worry. The farm had always been a place of safety, but now it felt like they were under siege from forces they didn't fully understand.

"What if this is the last warning we get?" she asked softly. Daniel reached for her hand, squeezing it gently. "Then we'll be ready."

Just as they were about to end the meeting, there was a loud crash outside, followed by Bear's furious barking. Everyone shot to their feet, rushing toward the door.

"What now?" Daniel muttered, grabbing his rifle as he led the way outside. The scene that greeted them sent a wave of fear through the group. A large object—a rock, wrapped in a piece of bloodied cloth—lay in the middle of the yard. As Daniel stepped closer, he saw that the cloth had been torn from someone's shirt, and scrawled across it in jagged letters were the words: "You've been warned. This is only the beginning."

Maggie's heart pounded as she stared at the bloodied message, her hands trembling. The threats had just turned deadly.

Chapter Thirty-Six: A Reckoning

The town of Briarwood seemed quieter than usual as Clara unlocked the door to Hartwell Mercantile, her hands moving with practiced ease as she prepared the store for another day. The morning sun streamed through the windows, casting a warm glow over the neatly arranged shelves. The store had become a second home for her, a place of peace amidst the storm of tension brewing over the past few weeks. Outside, Bear sat patiently by the door, his sharp eyes scanning the street, always alert. The faithful dog had been on edge ever since the incident with the Townsend brothers, constantly vigilant.

Inside, Maggie was busy in the back, counting supplies and organizing stock.

"You ready for today, Clara?" she called, her voice tinged with the same unease everyone seemed to feel.

Clara adjusted the display of fresh flowers on the counter, her hands moving quickly but her mind wandering.

"I think so. But after what happened with Nathan Townsend last night, I can't help but feel like something's coming."

Maggie emerged from the back, wiping her hands on her apron. "You're not alone in that. We've all been on edge, but Daniel's out at the farm with Hank, Pete, and Sam. Whatever happens, we'll be ready."

Clara nodded, though the tension gnawing at her didn't ease. "I just hope this is the last of it."

Across town, a storm was brewing, and it wasn't just the weather. Word had spread quickly about the latest threats from the Townsend family, and Sheriff Turner was on high alert, patrolling the streets with Deputy Sullivan.

Out at Whitaker Farm, Daniel stood with his men, overseeing the repairs. Though scarred from the fire, the barn was slowly restored to its former glory. Hank, Pete, and Sam were hard at work but shared a sense of foreboding. Willow grazed peacefully nearby, seemingly unaware of the tension, while Bear patrolled the property, ever watchful.

"Feels like we're waitin' for somethin' to break," Pete muttered as he nailed a final plank into place.

Standing nearby with his rifle slung over his shoulder, Hank nodded grimly.

"They're not done with us yet. I can feel it."

Their conversation was cut short by the distant sound of hooves thundering down the road. Sam, keeping watch near the farm's entrance, turned toward the approaching dust cloud, his heart sinking as he recognized the figures leading the charge.

"It's them," Sam called out, his voice tense. "The Townsends."

Daniel's jaw tightened as he spotted the familiar figures of Jonathan and Nathan Townsend, riding hard toward the farm with a group of men in tow. The final showdown had arrived. Back at the store, Clara had just finished helping a customer when the door swung open, and Sheriff Turner stepped inside, his face set in a grim expression.

"Clara, Maggie, you need to come with me. Now." Maggie's heart leaped into her throat. "What's going on?"

"The Townsends are heading for the farm. Daniel and the others are outnumbered, and I don't want you two anywhere near it if things go south."

Maggie didn't hesitate. "We're coming with you."

Clara, though her hands shook slightly, grabbed her shawl and hurried to follow Maggie. Bear, sensing the urgency in the air, was already on his feet, barking as if he knew what was coming. As they made their way through town, the air felt thick with anticipation. Whispers of what was happening had spread like wildfire, and the people of Briarwood had begun to gather in small groups, talking in hushed voices. When they arrived at Whitaker Farm, the scene that greeted them sent a shiver down Clara's spine.

Daniel stood firm in front of the barn, rifle in hand, flanked by Hank, Pete, and Sam. Across from them, Jonathan Townsend sat on his horse, his face twisted with fury, while Nathan lingered behind him, looking uneasy.

"You think you can just take what's ours and get away with it?" Jonathan snarled, his hand twitching near the gun at his side. Daniel's voice was calm, but the tension in the air was palpable.

"This was never yours to take, Jonathan. It doesn't have to end this way."

Nathan shifted in his saddle, his eyes darting nervously between his brother and Daniel. "Jonathan, maybe it's time we—"

"Shut up, Nathan!" Jonathan snapped, his fury boiling over.

"They've taken everything from us!" Before anyone could move, the sound of more hooves echoed in the distance. Sheriff Turner, leading a group of townspeople, arrived just in time. They quickly fanned out, forming a protective line behind Daniel and his men.

"This is over, Jonathan," the sheriff called out, his voice steady but firm. "The people of Briarwood won't let you destroy this farm or this town any longer."

For a long moment, Jonathan's hand hovered near his gun. His face twisted with rage, but he knew the odds were no longer in his favor. Slowly, he glanced over at Nathan, who was staring at the ground, his expression full of regret.

"It's over," Nathan said softly, his voice trembling. "Let's go."

Jonathan hesitated, but the fire in his eyes had dimmed. Without a word, he turned his horse and rode away, his brothers following closely behind. The Townsend reign of terror had finally come to an end.

As the dust settled, a collective sigh of relief washed over everyone. Maggie ran to Daniel, throwing her arms around him, her heart racing with fear and joy.

"It's over," she whispered, her voice trembling with emotion. Daniel held her close, his breath steadying as he kissed her forehead. "We made it through."

Nearby, Clara stood with Pete, her heart still racing but a smile playing on her lips.

"I never thought it would end like this." Pete wrapped an arm around her shoulders, his own relief palpable.

"Neither did I. But it's a new start, Clara. For all of us." Sam, standing nearby, gave a satisfied nod as he watched the last of the Townsends disappear over the horizon. "It's about time."

That evening, as the farm settled into a peaceful quiet, Maggie and Daniel sat by the fire inside their farmhouse. Bear lay at their feet, finally at ease, while Willow grazed outside the window under the moon's soft light.

"It feels strange, doesn't it?" Maggie asked softly, her fingers intertwined with Daniel's. "Like we've been waiting for the other shoe to drop, but now it's done."

Daniel nodded, his expression softening. "It's strange, but it's over now. And now we can move forward—without the Townsends looming over us."

Maggie smiled, resting her head on his shoulder. The future, once clouded with uncertainty, finally felt bright. As they sat together, wrapped in each other's warmth, the stars above twinkled in the clear night sky as if promising peace and new beginnings.

Chapter Thirty-Seven: A Promise of Tomorrow

The following morning, Briarwood woke to a quiet calm that had not been felt in weeks. The tension that had gripped the town ever since the Townsend family began their campaign of sabotage was gone, replaced by a sense of peace. The shadows that had lingered over Whitaker Farm and Hartwell Mercantile had finally lifted. Inside the farmhouse, Maggie stood by the window, watching as the early morning sun cast golden light over the fields. Willow wandered through the paddock, while Bear sat on the porch, his ears twitching as he watched over the peaceful scene. The feeling of safety, of finally being able to breathe, was almost overwhelming. Daniel appeared behind her, wrapping his arms around her waist.

"You're up early," he murmured, kissing her lips softly. Maggie leaned into him, her heart feeling lighter than it had in months.

"I couldn't sleep. It feels like everything's finally… right again." Daniel rested his chin on her shoulder, looking out at the land they had fought so hard to protect.

"It is. The Townsends are gone, and we can finally focus on the future."

Maggie smiled, her thoughts drifting to the wedding. "It feels like we've been waiting forever for this. I almost can't believe it's really happening."

Daniel turned her around to face him, his eyes filled with love and relief.

"It's happening, Maggie. And nothing is going to stop us now."

Meanwhile, over at Hartwell Mercantile, Clara was already hard at work, organizing the store and setting up new displays. After weeks of uncertainty and tension, returning to the normal rhythm of daily life felt like a breath of fresh air. The bell over the door jingled, and Clara looked up to see Pete walking in, his usual grin firmly in place.

"Morning, Clara. How's the store holding up?"

Clara smiled as she dusted off a nearby shelf. "It's nice to be back to normal. I feel like I can actually breathe in here again."

Pete leaned against the counter, watching her with a fond smile. "You look happier today. I was worried about you yesterday."

Clara laughed softly, her cheeks flushing. "I was worried about everyone yesterday."

"Fair enough," Pete replied, his tone turning serious for a moment. "But you did good, Clara. All of us made it through, and now we can focus on what's ahead."

Clara looked up from her work, her eyes meeting Pete's. For a moment, they simply stood there, the weight of all they'd been through hanging in the air between them. But instead of the fear and uncertainty that had defined the last few weeks, there was now only hope.

"What's ahead for us, Pete?" Clara asked softly, a smile tugging at her lips. Pete's grin returned, a spark of mischief in his eyes.

"Well, I was thinkin' you, and I might start planning something of our own—once Maggie and Daniel are hitched, of course."

Clara's heart skipped a beat, but before she could respond, the door opened again, and Maggie stepped inside, carrying a basket of fresh flowers.

"Good morning!" Maggie called, her voice filled with energy and excitement.

"I thought I'd bring some flowers from the farm to brighten up the store." Clara smiled, grateful for the interruption, though her mind still swirled with Pete's words.

"They're beautiful, Maggie. The store could use a little color after everything that's happened."

Pete winked at Clara before heading toward the back of the store to help organize supplies. Maggie, noticing the subtle exchange, raised an eyebrow but said nothing, choosing instead to help Clara arrange the flowers.

"How are you feeling about the wedding?" Clara asked as they worked side by side. "It's coming up so fast."

"I'm excited," Maggie said, her smile soft and genuine. "For the first time in a while, I feel like everything is falling into place. The farm's safe, the store's back on track, and Daniel and I can finally get married without looking over our shoulders."

Clara nodded, her own heart swelling with happiness for her friend. "It's going to be perfect, Maggie. You deserve this."

Maggie glanced toward the back of the store, where Pete was working. "And what about you and Pete? I saw that little exchange earlier."

Clara's cheeks flushed, but she couldn't suppress the smile across her face. "He mentioned… planning something. But I'm not sure what he meant."

Maggie grinned, her eyes sparkling with amusement. "I think I have an idea of what he's planning. But I'll let him surprise you."

As the day wore on, preparations for the wedding continued steadily. Hank, Sam, and Pete had spent the morning setting up benches and lanterns around the barn for the ceremony. The townspeople had offered their help, and soon, the farm was a flurry of activity—decorating, cooking, and preparing for what promised to be a beautiful day. The sound of laughter filled the air as children ran through the fields, playing tag while their parents worked together to finish the final touches. The heavy burden that had hung over the farm for so long had finally lifted, replaced by the lightness of community and celebration. Daniel stood with Hank, watching as the decorations took shape.

"I never thought we'd get here," Daniel said quietly, his eyes sweeping over the farm.

Hank chuckled, patting Daniel on the back. "It's been a long road, but you made it. You and Maggie are gonna have the life you've been fightin' for."

Daniel smiled, his heart full. "Yeah, we will."

That evening, as the sun set over Whitaker Farm, Daniel and Maggie took a quiet walk along the edge of the fields, Bear trotting faithfully by their side. The day had been filled with activity and preparations, but now, with the stars beginning to twinkle in the sky, they allowed themselves a moment of stillness.

"I can't believe it's tomorrow," Maggie said softly, her hand in Daniel's.

"Neither can I," Daniel replied, squeezing her hand gently. "But I wouldn't change a thing."

They stopped at the old oak tree where they had shared so many quiet moments, and for a while, they stood in silence, watching as the fireflies blinked lazily through the air.

"I love you, Maggie," Daniel said, his voice low and filled with emotion. "And tomorrow, we'll start the rest of our lives together."

Maggie smiled, her heart overflowing with love. "I love you too, Daniel. Tomorrow can't come soon enough."

As the night settled in and the farm grew quiet, Maggie and Daniel sat on the porch, watching the stars. The peaceful night felt like a promise of the happiness that lay ahead. Inside, Clara and Pete worked quietly, making sure everything was set for the next day. Pete glanced over at Clara, a small smile tugging at the corner of his lips.

"Tomorrow's gonna be perfect," Pete said softly, stepping closer to Clara.

Clara looked up at him, her heart fluttering. "It is."

"And maybe, once this is all over, we can start thinkin' about our own future," Pete added, his voice warm and full of hope.

Clara smiled, her heart swelling with happiness. "I'd like that."

Chapter Thirty-Eight: A Celebration of Love

The morning of the wedding dawned with clear skies and the soft warmth of the sun filtering through the trees at Whitaker Farm. The hustle and bustle of preparation finally gave way to an air of calm anticipation. It was the perfect day for Maggie and Daniel to begin the rest of their lives together. Standing in front of the mirror in Maggie's room, Clara adjusted the delicate lavender ribbon on her dress. Her hands shook slightly with excitement, her heart full as she prepared to take her place as Maggie's maid of honor. The soft fabric of the dress swayed around her feet, the color complementing her glowing complexion.

"Maggie, you look beautiful," Clara said as she turned to face her friend, standing in front of the full-length mirror. Maggie's wedding gown was simple but elegant, the ivory lace flowing softly to the floor. Her dark hair, braided with small sprigs of lavender, cascaded down her back, and her blue eyes sparkled with joy and nerves.

"Thank you," Maggie said, her voice barely above a whisper. "I can't believe this day is finally here."

Clara smiled, stepping forward to squeeze Maggie's hand gently.

"It's going to be perfect. Daniel's waiting for you, and everyone's gathered to celebrate. You're so loved, Maggie."

Maggie took a deep breath, her heart racing as the moment finally hit her. "I'm ready."

Down by the old oak tree near the pond, the ceremony was about to begin. The townspeople had gathered in quiet excitement, their voices hushed as they took their seats on the benches that lined the grassy clearing. Lanterns hung from the branches, casting a warm glow over the scene, and wildflowers bloomed in soft bouquets around the altar. Pete, standing beside Daniel as his best man, couldn't help but feel a swell of pride as he looked at his friend. Daniel had never seemed more at peace, his face happy as he waited for Maggie to arrive. Hank, Sam, and many stood nearby, all smiles as they shared in the moment.

"You ready for this?" Pete asked with a teasing grin, though his voice was warm with genuine affection. Daniel chuckled, his eyes never leaving the path where Maggie would soon appear.

"More than ready."

The soft sound of music began to fill the air as Bear, who had been sitting patiently by the front, perked up his ears. All eyes turned toward the path, and a hush fell over the gathering. Maggie appeared, her arm linked with Sheriff Turner, who had kindly offered to walk her down the aisle. Her gaze met Daniel's, and the rest of the world seemed to disappear for a moment. Only him was waiting for her with love and devotion in his eyes. Standing beside Maggie as her maid of honor,

Clara felt tears prick the corners of her eyes as she watched the couple's joy radiate across the clearing. As Maggie reached Daniel, the sheriff gently squeezed her hand before stepping aside. The two stood facing each other, their hands entwined, as the officiant began the ceremony.

The vows were simple, heartfelt, and filled with love.

"I never thought I'd find someone who understood me so completely," Maggie said, her voice soft but steady as she looked into Daniel's eyes. "But from the moment we met, you've been my strength, peace, and heart. Today, I promise to stand by your side through every storm and every sunrise for the rest of my life."

Daniel's eyes glistened with emotion as he spoke. "Maggie, you've brought light to my life in ways I never imagined. You're my home, my heart, and my greatest joy. Today, I promise to love, protect, and walk beside you, no matter what comes our way. You're everything to me."

As the officiant pronounced them husband and wife, Daniel leaned in, pressing a tender kiss to Maggie's lips as the gathering erupted in applause and cheers. Bear barked joyfully, wagging his tail, and Willow, tied nearby, let out a soft whinny as if sensing the joy of the moment.

After the ceremony, the farm came alive with celebration. As the townspeople gathered to share in the couple's happiness, tables had been set up around the barn, filled with food and drink. Laughter and conversation filled the air, and the smell of fresh bread and roasted meats wafted through the gathering. Clara stood with Pete, watching Daniel and Maggie dance together under the twinkling lanterns. There was peace and joy in the air that Clara hadn't felt in a long time.

"They look happy," Clara said softly, smiling as Maggie laughed and twirled in Daniel's arms.

"They are," Pete replied, his voice warm as he watched the couple. "And they deserve every bit of it."

Clara glanced up at Pete, her heart fluttering as she caught the soft expression on his face. She had grown closer to him over the past weeks, and now, standing here with him, she felt something shift between them. As the night grew darker and the stars twinkled overhead, Pete gently took Clara's hand and led her away from the crowd. They walked quietly toward the edge of the fields, where the night sky stretched above them in a blanket of shimmering stars.

"Clara," Pete began, his voice steady but filled with emotion. "I've been thinkin' about this for a while now, and after everything we've been through, I know one thing for sure."

Clara's heart pounded as she turned to face him, her hand still held in his. Pete took a deep breath, his eyes locking onto hers with a tenderness she had never seen before.

"I love you, Clara. And I don't want to wait any longer to ask you... will you marry me?" Clara's breath caught in her throat, her eyes filling with tears of joy as she nodded.

"Yes, Pete. Yes, I will."

With a broad smile, Pete pulled her into his arms, pressing a soft kiss to her lips as the stars above seemed to shine just a little brighter.

As the celebration continued late into the night, the farm was filled with laughter, music, and the warm glow of lanterns. Maggie and Daniel danced together under the stars, surrounded by the people they loved, their hearts full and their future bright. Pete and Clara, too, found themselves wrapped in the joy of the evening, their newfound engagement adding a layer of magic to the night. And as the townspeople finally began to disperse and the quiet of the night settled in once more, Whitaker Farm stood as a place of love, unity, and hope—a place where new beginnings were always possible.

Chapter Thirty-Nine: New Horizons

The morning after the wedding, Whitaker Farm was quiet, the remnants of the celebration still scattered across the yard. The soft golden light of dawn filtered through the trees, casting long shadows across the fields. Bear, still loyal as ever, lay on the porch, his head resting on his paws, watching the peaceful scene. Inside the farmhouse, Maggie awoke with a contented sigh, her body still wrapped in the warmth of the blankets and Daniel's embrace. The world outside seemed calm for the first time in what felt like forever. The weight of the past few months—the threats, the uncertainty, the fear—had lifted. The quiet, steady certainty of love and the future they had fought so hard to build was in its place.

"Good morning, Mrs. Whitaker," Daniel murmured sleepily, his voice a low rumble against her ear. Maggie smiled, the sound of his voice filling her with joy.

"Good morning, Mr. Whitaker."

They lay there in the stillness for a while, the world outside waiting for them to join it, but neither of them was in any hurry. It felt too good, too right, to be here together, finally able to breathe in the newness of their life as husband and wife.

When they finally made their way downstairs, the kitchen was filled with the soft sounds of breakfast being prepared. Clara and Pete were already up, moving around the kitchen easily. Their movements synchronized as if they had been doing this together for years. The warmth of the fire and the smell of fresh coffee filled the air.

"Morning," Clara called out, her face glowing with happiness. She wore the same soft smile that had been there since the night before, the sparkle of her new engagement ring catching the morning light as she poured coffee for everyone. Maggie's eyes twinkled as she took a seat at the table.

"Good morning. How does it feel, Clara, to be the future Mrs.?" Clara's cheeks flushed, and she exchanged a glance with Pete before answering.

"It feels… wonderful," she said softly, her voice full of emotion. Pete grinned from across the room, his hands busy kneading dough for the bread.

"We figured if it worked for you two, we oughta try our luck."

Daniel chuckled, taking a seat beside Maggie and reaching for his coffee.

"Looks like the farm's gonna be filled with weddings before long."

Later that day, as Maggie and Clara returned to Hartwell Mercantile, the peaceful energy from the morning stayed with them. Their walk into town was filled with a quiet conversation about the future—about what Maggie and Daniel would do next and about Clara's excitement for her own upcoming wedding.

"I still can't believe it," Clara said as they neared the store. "After everything that happened with the Townsends, we'd never have a moment of peace again."

Maggie nodded, her expression thoughtful. "It feels like a new beginning. But I think we're stronger because of what we went through. We had the town behind us, which we'll never take for granted."

As they unlocked the doors to Hartwell Mercantile, Maggie felt a wave of gratitude wash over her. The store, their community, and their families had all weathered the storm. Now, it was time to look forward. Inside the store, the familiar sounds of their daily routine resumed. Customers came and went, congratulating Maggie on her marriage and Clara on her engagement. The flow of life in Briarwood had returned, steady and comforting.

Meanwhile, back at Whitaker Farm, Daniel, Pete, and the farmhands—Hank and Sam—were already back to work, the buzz of activity filling the air. Though the day before had been filled with celebration, the responsibilities of the farm never ceased, and Daniel knew there was much to be done. Pete worked alongside Daniel, his eyes occasionally drifting to the ring on his finger, a soft smile playing on his lips.

The promise of a future with Clara filled his heart with joy, but he was also mindful of the work that lay ahead.

"Hank, make sure we get the fences repaired before the next storm rolls in," Daniel called, keeping an eye on the fields.

The damage from the last bout of bad weather was still being patched up.

"Got it, boss," Hank replied, heading toward the western field with Sam close behind. Pete, catching the look of determination on Daniel's face, set down his tools for a moment.

"You think we'll ever really be done fixin' up this place?"

Daniel chuckled. "I don't think a farm's ever really 'done,' Pete. But as long as we keep pushing forward, we'll get there."

The two men stood in comfortable silence for a moment, surveying the land that had become more than just a place to work—it was a symbol of everything they had built together with their families and friends.

As the day drew to a close, Maggie and Daniel found themselves once again on the porch, watching the sun dip below the horizon. The sky was painted in shades of orange and pink, the soft breeze carrying the sounds of the farm animals settling down for the night.

"It feels strange, doesn't it?" Maggie asked softly, leaning against Daniel as they sat on the porch swing. "To have everything so… peaceful."

Daniel nodded, his hand resting on hers. "After everything we've been through, I guess we're not used to things being calm."

Maggie looked up at him, her blue eyes filled with a quiet determination. "Do you think it'll stay this way?"

Daniel thought for a moment before answering. "I don't know. But whatever comes our way, I know we can face it. Together."

Maggie smiled, resting her head against his shoulder as the night grew darker, the stars beginning to twinkle above them. The world around them might change, but the love they had found and the community they had built would always be their foundation.

Later that evening, Clara and Pete joined them on the porch, settling into the quiet of the night. Pete leaned back in his chair, his arm draped around Clara's shoulders as they looked out over the fields, the sounds of the farm lulling them into a peaceful calm.

"You ever think about what's next?" Pete asked, his voice soft but thoughtful.

Clara smiled, her head resting against his chest. "I think about it all the time."

"And?" Pete asked, a playful smile tugging at his lips.

Clara looked up at him, her eyes twinkling in the dim light.

"I think the future is exactly what we make of it." Daniel and Maggie exchanged glances, smiling at Clara's words' simple truth. The future, once clouded with uncertainty, now seemed wide open, filled with possibilities they could never have imagined.

Chapter Forty: The Final Reckoning

It had been two months since the Townsends had been driven from Hartwood, and life had slowly returned to normal. The farm was thriving, the townspeople were united, and Maggie and Daniel had begun to look toward the future with hope. But in the back of Maggie's mind, there was always a lingering shadow—the knowledge that the Townsends wouldn't forget what had happened.

At Hartwell Mercantile, Clara and Maggie were busy stocking shelves and preparing for the day. It was a peaceful afternoon, the kind where the everyday routine of life lulled them into a sense of calm. The sun filtered through the windows, casting a warm glow over the store.

But the peace was shattered when the door creaked open, and a figure stepped inside. Jonathan Townsend. His eyes were dark, cold, and filled with a deadly purpose. He had returned for revenge, and the look on his face sent a chill down Maggie's spine.

"Maggie Whitaker," Jonathan growled, his voice low and menacing. "Did you really think you could ruin my family and not pay for it?"

Maggie's breath caught in her throat, her heart racing as she stepped back. She had expected this in some distant part of her mind, but seeing him now, standing in the doorway with fury in his eyes, made the threat all too real.

"What do you want, Jonathan?" Maggie asked, her voice shaking.

Jonathan's lips curled into a cruel smile. "I want you to pay for what you did."

Clara, who had been arranging stock near the back of the store, froze when she heard Jonathan's voice. Her eyes darted to Maggie, then to the revolver she kept hidden behind the counter for emergencies. She had always hoped she'd never have to use it, but now, as she saw the murderous intent in Jonathan's eyes, she knew there was no choice.

"Get away from her," Clara called out, stepping forward, her hand hovering near the hidden revolver.

Jonathan sneered, taking a threatening step toward Maggie. "Or what? You think you can stop me?"

Maggie's heart raced as she took another step back, but her mind was already working, scanning the store for any way to escape or defend herself. The door seemed too far, and Jonathan's eyes were wild, filled with rage and vengeance. Just as Jonathan lunged forward, reaching for Maggie, Clara's hand shot out, pulling the revolver from its hiding place. In a heartbeat, she aimed at Jonathan, her hands steady despite the fear coursing through her veins.

"Stop," Clara warned, her voice sharp and firm.

But Jonathan didn't stop. His eyes narrowed, and with a snarl, he moved toward Maggie with deadly intent. Clara didn't hesitate. She pulled the trigger. The shot echoed through the small store, shattering the silence and sending birds scattering from the nearby trees.

Jonathan stumbled back, a look of shock on his face as he clutched his chest, blood seeping through his fingers. He staggered, his breath ragged, before collapsing onto the floor. Maggie stood frozen, her eyes wide with shock, her hands trembling. She had never expected Clara to fire, never thought it would come to this. Clara lowered the revolver, her heart pounding in her chest as she stared at Jonathan's lifeless body. Her hands shook, but her mind was clear—she had done what she had to do to protect her friend. Moments later, the sound of galloping hooves reached their ears.

Sheriff Turner, who had heard the shot from his nearby office, arrived at the store in seconds. He burst through the door, his eyes scanning the scene.

"What happened?" the sheriff demanded, his voice urgent.

Clara, calm despite the adrenaline rushing through her, looked at him with steady eyes. "He came for Maggie. He was going to kill her. I had no choice."

The sheriff looked down at Jonathan's body, then at Clara. His expression softened as he realized the gravity of the situation.

"You did what you had to do."

As the sheriff took charge of the scene, the townspeople gathered outside the store, whispers spreading quickly about what had happened. Maggie, still shaken, sat in a chair, her hands clasped tightly together as she tried to steady her breath. Clara stood beside her, her hand resting gently on her shoulder.

"It's over now, Maggie. He can't hurt you anymore."

Maggie looked up at Clara, her eyes filled with gratitude and disbelief. "I can't believe you... you saved my life."

Clara gave her a small, reassuring smile. "I told you—I'll always have your back."

As the sheriff and his deputies worked to clear the scene, Daniel arrived, his face pale with worry as he rushed to Maggie's side.

"Maggie!" Daniel knelt beside her, his hands gently cupping her face. "Are you all right?"

Maggie nodded, though her voice trembled as she spoke. "I'm okay. Clara... she saved me."

Daniel glanced up at Clara, his eyes filled with gratitude. "Thank you."

Clara gave a quiet nod, the weight of the moment settling over her as the adrenaline began to fade. She had done what she needed to do, but the gravity of it still lingered.

The following days were quiet, as Briarwood processed the shock of Jonathan Townsend's return and the violence that had followed. The sheriff's investigation confirmed Clara's actions as self-defense, and no charges were filed.

town, once again, rallied around Maggie and Clara, offering their support and assurance. The dark cloud that had hung over them for so long had finally lifted, and life began to return to normal.

One evening, as the sun set over Whitaker Farm, Maggie, Daniel, Clara, and Pete sat together on the porch, watching the sky turn shades of orange and pink. The peace that had been so elusive for so long now felt real—tangible.

Maggie turned to Clara, her heart full of gratitude. "I don't know how to thank you." Clara smiled softly, her gaze fixed on the horizon. "You don't have to thank me, Maggie. We're family. And family takes care of each other."

The warmth of their bond and shared experiences filled the air as the night settled in. The dangers of the past were behind them, and the future was bright—filled with hope, love, and the strength of their community.